Course in
Isaac Pitman Shorthand

NEW ERA EDITION

TORONTO: CANADA
THE COMMERCIAL TEXT-BOOK COMPANY

———

SIR ISAAC PITMAN & SONS, LTD.
70 BOND STREET, TORONTO
and at London, Bath, Melbourne, and New York

PRINTED IN GREAT BRITAIN
AT THE PITMAN PRESS, BATH

PREFACE

THE first edition of this work met with the warm approbation of teachers and students, and its popularity was firmly established at once.

This New Era Edition embodies many improvements and represents another forward step in shorthand textbook planning. Each principle is simply stated and profusely illustrated. When such explanation is desirable, the cautions to be observed in the use of that principle are explained. Exercises are introduced in each lesson at every point that requires application drill. These exercises consist of word lists, groups of sentences and brief business letters, all of which, in their construction, indicate a radical departure from the usual exercise matter, for special attention has been centered on the acquisition of a varied vocabulary, the development of ease in note-taking ability, and on the proper provision for a cumulative review of the theory.

Another unique departure is to be found in the elimination from the lists of word-signs of all words that cannot strictly be included in that classification, together with those words that are of infrequent occurrence in ordinary conversation or correspondence.

Several improvements, the usefulness of which has been amply tested and fully demonstrated, have also been incorporated in the principles of the theory. They include, among the more important of these, slight modifications in the use of the Tick *H* and the Reverse Form of *Fl*; Position Writing according to the first vowel sound in the word; a restricted use of the *W* Semicircle, and a discontinuance of the *Y* Semicircle. One or two additional minor changes will also be noted.

To supplement these various improvements there have been added, at the end of the text, thirty-seven pages of business letters in the most approved modern style, and short articles in engraved shorthand, which will serve as the connecting link in passing gradually from the study of the theory to the acquisition of speed in shorthand writing. This feature will appeal strongly to all teachers.

The publishers herewith express their sincere appreciation of the many helpful suggestions so kindly offered by teachers and reporters everywhere. Their deep interest in and loyalty to the Isaac Pitman System of Shorthand have made this work possible.

ISAAC PITMAN SHORTHAND

A BRIEF HISTORICAL SKETCH

IN 1837 Isaac Pitman published his first system of shorthand under the title of " Stenographic Sound Hand." After fifteen years of teaching, lecturing and studying, the system was perfected to such a degree that in 1852 it met every requirement of the high speed writer, as well as the needs of the ordinary business man. The extraordinary popularity it attained was well deserved, for it was by far the simplest and the most practicable system of shorthand writing that had ever been invented.

Isaac's three brothers co-operated with him in the spread of his system, and Benn, in 1853, brought the invention of his brother to the United States. The Benn Pitman " Manual of Phonography " appeared in 1855, and was shortly afterwards followed by the Andrew J. Graham, James E. Munson, and several other less commonly known " systems." The deviations in these texts from the original Isaac Pitman system were so slight and so unimportant that to characterize them as " distinctive systems " is as misleading as it is unfair to the inventor of Pitmanic Shorthand.

During this period, Isaac Pitman Shorthand was undergoing a continued process of growth and development, and many improvements were incorporated in the principles. The phenomenal growth of the system throughout Great Britain spread to America and Canada, and, steadily forging to the front, it is to-day recognized as the universal system

Distinguishing Features

What are the distinguishing features of this system that make it so practicable for all purposes and requirements ?

1. An alphabet which provides a sign for every primary sound in the English language.

2. The geometric characters used to represent the consonant sounds lend themselves very readily to Angular joinings. The superiority of such joinings for reading purpose has never been questioned. *Blends* are dispensed with, and so are the constant changes of hand direction occasioned by the writing of numerous curved signs taking opposite directions. Thus retardation of hand movement and illegibility of outline are minimized, while labyrinthian twists and turns are avoided.

3. A series of abbreviations, consisting of circles, hooks, loops, and other simple devices, is employed for the secondary representation of the more frequently recurring consonant sounds and natural combinations of consonant sounds in the language. By this means the amount of actual writing is reduced to the lowest possible minimum, and every consonant sound in the word is represented. There is no need for recourse to the doubtful expedient of lopping off parts of words, at the writer's pleasure, when long words are to be represented.

4. Strict adherence to the phonetic structure of the language is closely followed. Words are not " butchered " to fit the needs of a faulty scheme of sound representation.

5. Word-signs, in the strict sense of the term, are so few as to be negligible in number. Stress is placed on a *rational* application of the *principles* of the system for the proper representation of words in shorthand, and not upon the memorization of hundreds upon hundreds of *special* word-signs.

6. Position Writing. This is a simple and effective device that enhances the legibility of the outline and is highly prized by the fastest writers in the world as an invaluable aid.

7. Hand lifts are the exception and not the rule. Greater rapidity and ease of reading are the direct results.

In addition, several clearly defined and easily understood guiding principles of hand motion determine the formation of outlines. Similar guiding principles make the written outline easy to read. Every possible contingency is provided for ; nothing is left to chance.

It is this scientific development of the Isaac Pitman System, based on the phonetic structure and demands of the English Language, that clothes it with a value always recognized and not to be found in so-called light-line, connective-vowel systems.

The System of Achievements

No other system of shorthand has produced so many high speed writers. Long before the Civil War, Dennis F. Murphy began reporting the Senate debates in Pitman Shorthand, and for forty years his shorthand notes were transcribed by others. The Lincoln-Douglas debates were reported by Robert R. Hitt in Pitman Shorthand, and his notes also were, for the most part, transcribed by his office assistants. Never was it necessary for Mr. Lincoln in his official edition of these debates to make any changes in the original transcription.

From that time to the present day, Pitman Shorthand has been the instrument for recording practically all public speaking in the English language. Pitman Shorthand is used by all the Congressional reporters in Washington, and all the recent world conferences were reported in Pitman Shorthand. More than 90 per cent of the Court reporters in the United States write Pitman Shorthand.

What one Pitman Writer, Mr. Behrin, has accomplished

February 2, 1911. Passed Civil Service Examination for Official Court Stenographer with 100 per cent. rating. He wrote 200 words a minute for five minutes with absolute accuracy.

1911, 1912, 1913 *and* 1914. Won the title, " Champion Shorthand Writer of the World " in open contest four successive times, and retired from these contests.

December, 1919. Wrote for two minutes at 324 words a minute, with only two minor errors, in a contest held by the New York State Shorthand Reporters' Association. This was the first time that more than three hundred words a minute had been written and transcribed publicly.

December, 1920. Won New York State Championship, writing 240 words a minute for five minutes, with only one error ; 280 words a minute for five minutes, with only three errors.

August, 1922. Made a brilliant come-back in the International
Contest, again winning the championship of the world. He
broke all records at the championship speeds of 200, 240 and
280 words a minute (five minute tests at each speed). His
average accuracy was 99.5 per cent, or 19 minor errors in 3,610
words. He eclipsed his own record of 98.3 per cent, made in
1913 at the same speeds. His performance was all the more
remarkable in view of the fact that he transcribed his notes in
less than half the allotted time.

TO THE STUDENT

You know full well that what is worth having is worth working for. Set yourself resolutely to the task you have begun, and you cannot fail. You are beginning the study of a subject that becomes more and more interesting and fascinating as you proceed. When you have acquired a mastery of Isaac Pitman Shorthand, you will possess a power by means of which untold numbers of young men and young women have won rapid and deserved promotion in all fields of endeavor. Everywhere you will find the successful business and professional man who made his start with shorthand. Prepare yourself thoroughly and diligently, and with the mastery of that art you will be ready for your march ONWARD and UPWARD.

Perseverance

Now and again you will meet with a problem which may appear more or less difficult. Make every effort to solve it yourself. If you are not successful, seek assistance. Your teacher will gladly give it to you. You will make your task more enjoyable, however, if you sweeten it with the pleasure and satisfaction of self-accomplishment. Under no circumstances should you pass on to a new point unless you understand clearly and thoroughly everything that has gone before.

Persevere in the early stages of your study, and soon you will have made a habit of the most important characteristic of the successful man or woman—*Perseverence*. Temper your perseverence with confidence. Develop a feeling of assurance in your own ability. It will forestall many seeming difficulties.

Do each day's task cheerfully and intelligently, without a feeling of anxiety or hurry. Bear in mind the ultimate goal, and remember that it can be attained only as the mountain peaks are reached by the climber. Progress must be slow and your footing sure. In every successful achievement you will find that it has been made possible by a due regard to details. It is with that feature of your study of shorthand that you must be specially concerned. There are many little details, which, if properly attended to, make your task a simpler one.

The Reading Habit

Nothing will help you to make progress more rapidly than the reading of shorthand notes. It not only enriches your vocabulary, but also develops your ability to apply the principles of the theory to the making of shorthand outlines. The Isaac Pitman System of Shorthand is known the world over for its wealth of literature, far in excess of all other systems combined. You may practise the reading of engraved shorthand while you are studying the theory of the system. The following titles give you an idea of the variety that is offered: *Aesop's Fables*; *Selected Readings* from American and English authors; *Gulliver's Voyage to Lilliput*; *The Return of Sherlock Holmes*; *Tales and Sketches* by Washington Irving; and many other similar works. In addition, there are numerous reading books in commercial correspondence. PITMAN'S JOURNAL (English Edition published weekly, American Edition published monthly), contains several pages of reading matter in each issue, aside from the many helpful suggestions given in other directions.

For the high speed aspirant, and for the ambitious shorthand student who seeks to enter the reporting field, there is also a wide choice of books, prepared especially for their needs. The *Isaac Pitman Dictation Course* is one of the most recent of the series of dictation texts, designed to assist the student to acquire speed in note-taking. Special contractions, phrases, and exercises are to be found in a series of *Phrase Books and Guides* covering practically every sphere of commercial and professional activity. There is no need that cannot be supplied.

Remember that achievement challenges achievement. Resolve, persevere, and aim high. Your success must follow.

THE FUNDAMENTAL PRINCIPLES OF
ISAAC PITMAN SHORTHAND

THE study of the theory of Isaac Pitman Shorthand takes on a more rational, and a more intensely interesting aspect when the student understands the reasons for the various devices employed. These reasons stand out clearly when the devices or rules of the system are analyzed in the light of the fundamental principles underlying the system. These fundamental principles are invariably the determining factors in the choice of an outline form.

Not only for the student of the theory of the system, but also for the speed aspirant, a clear understanding and ready application of these fundamental principles make for rapid and intelligent progress.

These fundamental principles deal with the FORM, LEGIBILITY, and BREVITY of the outlines from the standpoint of—

(a) Ease in writing, and (b) Ease in reading. Every outline should be subjected to each of these two *tests*.

FORM and BREVITY deal with the shorthand outline from the viewpoint of *ease* and *speed* in the *writing* of it.

LEGIBILITY deals with the shorthand outline from the viewpoint of—*ease* in the *reading* of it.

Form

Form takes cognizance, therefore, of—

(a) Angularity—wherever possible make and show clearly, sharp angles.

(b) Lineality—keep as close to the line of writing as possible.

(c) Forward Motion—prefer the forward motion of the hand to a backward motion.

(d) Similar or Continuous Motion—when joining strokes, keep the hand moving without a break, if possible. This avoids a change of direction and as a general rule gives a faster and better reading outline.

Legibility

LEGIBILITY deals with all the devices of the system which make for ease in the reading of an outline and requires a thorough understanding of—

(*a*) Balance or Symmetry—which means the preservation of the form of any consonant stroke so that its identity is not lost when joined to other strokes or modified by attachments, initial or final.

(*b*) Vocalization—which means the selection of that form of outline which can be vocalized to show all the vowel sounds heard in the word.

(*c*) Derivation—this principle takes note of the fact that derived forms of words should, wherever possible, be written like the primitives or the words from which they are derived.

(*d*) Vowel Indication—the presence or the absence of a vowel sound at a given place in the word is clearly indicated by the form of outline employed.

Brevity

BREVITY deals with the abbreviating devices employed in the system, and calls for the proper understanding of—

(*a*) Abbreviation—the various devices employed for shortening the writing of an outline by means of Circles, Loops and Hooks (small and large), and combinations of these, etc.

(*b*) Indication—the various means employed for indicating either a particular consonant sound, a group of consonant sounds, vowel sounds or words.

(*c*) Contractions—the various devices for representing long words. This includes all the word-signs, general and special, phrasing, omission of consonants in a few instances, etc.

As you study each device of the system, determine which of these fundamental principles prompted it.

INTRODUCTION

PITMAN SHORTHAND has been briefly but accurately described as " the art of representing spoken sounds by characters." What is the fundamental difference between shorthand characters and the letters in ordinary writing ?

Ordinary longhand spelling is seldom phonetic ; the English alphabet, consisting of twenty-six letters, cannot represent by distinct characters the thirty-six typical sounds of the language. Consequently, many of the letters are used to represent different sounds. *In Isaac Pitman Shorthand, however, a sign is provided for every sound in English, and words are written strictly according to sound.*

Two simple illustrations will demonstrate the difference between the ordinary and the phonetic spelling. (1) The *sounds* of the first consonant in the words *gem* and *game* are different, although they are represented in longhand by the same letter. *Gem* spelt phonetically is *j-e-m* ; the initial sound in *game* is *gay*. For these dissimilar sounds Pitman Shorthand provides dissimilar shorthand signs. (2) The vowel sounds heard in the words *tub* and *tube* are different. If the shorthand symbols were the equivalents of the letters of the common alphabet (the final *e* of tube being omitted because it is not sounded), each word would be written by the same characters, namely *t-u-b*. In shorthand, however, the different sounds *ŭ* and *ū* are indicated by different symbols.

The following illustrations will show the student how to spell when writing shorthand. Silent letters are omitted altogether.

palm would be spelt *pahm*	*coal* would be spelt *kōl*
pale ,, ,, ,, *pāl*	*door* ,, ,, ,, *dōr*
key ,, ,, ,, *kē*	*tomb* ,, ,, ,, *tōōm*
wrought ,, ,, ,, *rawt*	*knee* ,, ,, ,, *nē*

The shorthand characters should be made as neatly and as accurately as is possible. The signs join readily with one another, and they can be written at great speed when the rules are so familiar that they can be applied without hesitation. Resist the temptation to sacrifice neatness for speed. Speed in writing will follow neat and accurate practice naturally.

Attention is drawn to the meaning given to the terms *right motion* and *left motion* which occur in several of the lessons. By *right motion* is meant the motion taken by the hands of a clock, thus ; while *left motion* means the contrary motion, thus .

CONTENTS

xv

ISAAC PITMAN SHORTHAND NEW ERA COURSE

LESSON I

1. The First Eight Consonants. A consonant is a sound which cannot be produced distinctly without the aid of a vowel. The result of audible friction or stopping of the breath in some part of the mouth or throat is a consonant.

The first eight consonants are—

Letter	Character	Name	As sounded in	
P	\	pee	**p**ost	ro**p**e
B	\	bee	**b**oast	ro**b**e
T	|	tee	**t**ip	fa**t**e
D	|	dee	**d**ip	fa**d**e
CH	/	chay	**ch**est	e**tch**
J	/	jay	**j**est	e**dg**e
K	—	kay	**c**ane	lee**k**
G	—	gay	**g**ain	lea**g**ue

It will be observed that these consonants form pairs; thus, *p* and *b*, *t* and *d*, *ch* and *j*, *k* and *g*. The articulations in these pairs are the same, but the sound is light in the first consonant of each pair and heavy in the second. Each pair is represented by the same kind of stroke; but for the light sound a light stroke is written, and for the heavy sound a heavy stroke is written. Each sign represents one sound only and never under any circumstances represents any other sound.

The strokes *p, b, t, d, ch, j,* are written downward, and *k* and *g* horizontally, from left to right. They are *always* written in the same direction.

Practise these consonants until they can be written and read with ease.

2. The Dot Vowels. A vowel is a sound which can be produced without the assistance of any other. If the mouth-passage is left so open as not to cause audible friction, and voiced breath is sent through it, we have a vowel.

There are twelve simple vowel sounds in the English language. In Pitman Shorthand they are divided into two groups, six vowels represented by dots, and six represented by dashes.

A heavy dot represents the long vowels *ah, ā,* and *ē* as heard in the words *pa, bay, key* respectively. The corresponding short vowels, *ă, ĕ, ĭ,* as heard in the words *add, ebb,* and *pick* respectively, are represented by a light dot.

The chief difference between a short vowel and its corresponding long vowel is that the short vowel is more rapidly pronounced; thus,

The long vowel *ah* in *palm* pronounced quickly becomes the short vowel *ă* in *pat* ;

The long vowel *ā* in *pate* pronounced quickly becomes the short vowel *ĕ* in *pet* ;

The long vowel *ē* in *peat* pronounced quickly becomes the short vowel *ĭ* in *pit.*

3. Places of the Vowels. Alongside of each stroke are three places—*beginning, middle,* and *end*—in which to put the vowel-signs. The vowels are called *first, second,* or *third-place* vowels according to the place they occupy. The places of vowels are counted from the point where the stroke begins ; thus,

FIRST-PLACE DOT VOWELS—

ah, and the corresponding short *ă*, occupy first place, as

╲ *pa*, ╲ *bah*, 丨 *at*, 丨 *add*.

SECOND-PLACE DOT VOWELS—

ā, and the corresponding short *ĕ*, occupy second place, as

╲ *ape*, ╲ *bay*, — *ache*, — *egg*, / *edge*, / *etch*.

THIRD-PLACE DOT VOWELS—

ē, and the corresponding short *ĭ*, occupy third place, as

╲ *bee*, 丨 *eat*, / *each*, / *itch*, — *key*.

4. Vowels Before and After Consonants. A vowel may occur either before or after a consonant. An examination of the illustrations given in the preceding paragraph will show that if a vowel occurs before the consonant, the vowel-sign is written at the left-hand side of an upright or sloping stroke or above a horizontal stroke ; if the vowel occurs after the consonant, the vowel-sign is written at the right-hand side of an upright or sloping stroke or below a horizontal stroke. Compare—

Vowel before a Consonant	*Vowel after a Consonant*	*Vowel before a Consonant*	*Vowel after a Consonant*
丨 *eat*	丨 *tea*	丨 *at*	╲ *bee*
— *eke*	— *key*	— *egg*	╲ *pa*
/ *each*	/ *Gee*	╲ *Abe*	/ *jay*

Two short lines underneath an outline indicate an initial capital.

Exercise 1

Write in Shorthand. Each stroke should rest on the line.
Write the stroke first ; then put in the vowel-sign.

1. Aid, eight, ebb, ache, aitch.
2. Day, Tay, pay, Kay, gay.
3. Abe, bay, jay, age, etch.

5. The Position of Outlines. Just as there are three places in which to put the vowel-signs, so there are three positions in which to write the outlines of words. The *first* position is *above the line* ; the *second* position is *on the line* ; and the *third* position is *through the line*. The *first sounded vowel* in the word determines the position of the outline.

When the *first sounded vowel* in a word is a *first-place* vowel, the outline is written in the *first position* ; as

$\diagdown$ *pa*, $\diagdown$ *bah*, $|$ *at*, $|$ *add.*

When the *first sounded vowel* in a word is a *second-place* vowel, the outline is written in the *second position* ; as

$\diagdown$ *ape*, $\diagdown$ *bay*, $/$ *etch*, $|$ *Etta.*

When the *first sounded vowel* in a word is a *third-place* vowel, the outline is written in the *third position* ; as

$\diagdown$ *bee*, $|$ *eat*, $/$ *each*, $/$ *itch.*

Since it is not possible to write horizontal strokes through the line, there are only two positions for such consonants, namely, *above the line* for the *first position*, and *on the line* for the *second* and *third positions*.

Exercise 2

Write in Shorthand

1. Add, Addie, at, abbey.
2. Edge, ate, eddy, eighty, egg.
3. Tea, key, itchy, Edie, eke.

6. Joining of Consonants. Consonants are joined without lifting the pen, as in longhand. Begin the second where the first ends, and write the stroke in its proper direction—

⟍ *pt,* ＼ *pp,* ⟩ *pj,* ∟ *dk,* ⌐ *kd,* ∠ *ch k,* —— *gg,*
| *td,* —— *kg.*

7. Vowels Between Consonants. A first or a second-place vowel between two consonants is written *after the first* consonant in its proper place, and a third-place vowel is written *before the second* consonant in the third place ; thus,

⟍ *pad,* ∟ *take,* ∟ *tip,* —— *gag,* —— *cake,* —— *kick,*
| *date,* ⟍ *gap,* ⟍ *cape,* ⟍ *keep.*

Position Writing. It will be noticed from these illustrations that in outlines consisting of more than one consonant stroke, the *first downstroke* indicates the position.

Exercise 3

Read, copy, and transcribe

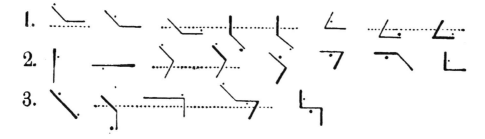

Write in Shorthand

4. Back, bake, beak, tack, take, tick, cheap, chip.
5. Teach, ditch, date, get, beg, kick, bet, bit.
6. Decay, pity, attach, attack, baggage.

8. Word-Signs. Abbreviated forms, known as word-signs, are provided for a number of frequently-occurring words. The words that are represented by these contracted signs are called *grammalogs* if one stroke is used, and *contractions* if more than one stroke is used. These word-signs will be a valuable aid to the student in the development of speed in writing shorthand, and should, therefore, be mastered thoroughly. In the longhand exercises which follow, the grammalogs and contractions are printed in italics.

9. Punctuation. A small cross × or long oblique line / indicates the period. The semicolon, the question mark, and the exclamation mark respectively are represented by these signs : ; ? ! The sign ↪ is employed to express a dash. Other punctuation marks are written in the usual manner.

GRAMMALOGS

a or *an*, *the* ; all, *too* or *two* ; *of*, *to* ; *on*, *but* ; (up) *and*, (up) *should* ; (down) *awe*, *aught*, or *ought*, *who* ; *put* ; *be*, *to be* ; *it*.

Exercise 4

Read, copy, and transcribe

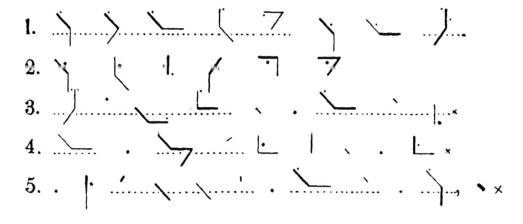

Write in Shorthand

6. Chap, jack, cap, peach, peak, peep, cheek.
7. Dig, gig, beet, agate, ditty, jab.
8. Keep *the* check, *but the* big debt *should be* paid.
9. *Put the* cage *on the* keg *and* take *the* package back.
10. Take *the* cheap bag back *to the* chap *who* paid.

Summary

1. In shorthand writing we write strictly according to the *sound* of words.

2. There are three places for vowel-signs and three positions for outlines of words. There are only two positions for horizontal strokes.

3. Vowel-signs are read before the consonant when placed at the left-hand side or above a consonant, and they are read after the consonant when placed on the right-hand side or below a consonant.

4. When consonants are joined, the second stroke begins where the first ends.

5. Between two strokes first and second-place vowels are written after the first stroke, and third-place vowels before the second stroke.

6. The first downstroke in an outline indicates the position.

LESSON II

10. The Second Eight Consonants. The second group of consonants, like the first group, consists of four pairs. Each curve has two forms, a light stroke to represent a light consonant, and a shaded stroke to represent the corresponding heavy sound.

Letter	Character	Name	As sounded in	
F	╲	ef	**fat**	**safe**
V	╲	vee	**vat**	sa**ve**
TH	(	ith	**th**igh	wrea**th**
TH	(	thee	**th**y	wrea**the**
S	)	ess	**seal**	ba**se**
Z	)	zee	**zeal**	bai**ze**
SH	⟋	ish	**sh**e	da**sh**
ZH	⟋	zhee	trea**s**ure	vi**s**ion

These are all downstrokes, though *sh* is written either upward or downward when it is joined to another stroke. It is more convenient to write it upward when it immediately precedes ╲ ╲ ((or ⌐ *l* (a sign which will be learned in the next and last group of consonants) ; and also when it immediately follows ╲ ╲ or | Practise these signs until they can be written and read with ease.

8

Exercise 5

Read, copy, and transcribe

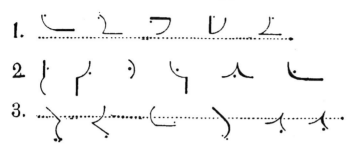

Write in Shorthand

4. Shah, path, cash, vat, asp.
5. Fed, fetch, they, bathe, shape.
6. Teeth, dizzy, feed, sheik, ease, easy.
7. Say, dish, if, fish, shake, sheaf.

11. **The Circle S.** The construction of the alphabet in Pitman Shorthand is such that a wealth of material is available for the formation of sound abbreviating devices. By the introduction of secondary shorthand characters words are fully represented in small, compact, and well-balanced outlines. These secondary characters are very simple. In this lesson one of them is introduced.

Besides the curve) for *s*, there is another sign for this frequently-occurring letter, namely, a small circle. This circle *s* is written (*a*) inside of a curve ; (*b*) outside of an angle ; and (*c*) with a left or backward motion to a straight stroke ; thus,

CIRCLE *S* INSIDE OF A CURVE—

     ⌣ *sf*, ⌣ *fs*, (*s th*, (*th s*,) *s sh*,) *sh s*.

CIRCLE *S* OUTSIDE OF AN ANGLE—

)⟩ *psj*, ⌐ *dsk*, ⟨ *jsp*, ⊤ *ksd*, ⟍ *gsp*.

CIRCLE *S* WITH A LEFT MOTION—

sb, *bs*, *st*, *ts*, *s ch*, *ch s*, *sk*, *ks*.

(*a*) At the beginning of an outline the circle *s* is written first and read first, and represents the sound of *s* only.

At the end of an outline the circle *s* is written last and read last. In the middle or at the end of an outline the circle represents the sound of either *s* or *z*.

INITIALLY, *spa*, *sip*, *zip*, *sake*, *ski*.

MEDIALLY, *desk*, *busied*, *passive*, *access*, *visit*, *evasive*.

FINALLY, *eats*, *teas*, *aches*, *gaze*, *geese*, *pays* or *pace*.

(*b*) Since the circle has no first, second, or third-place, vowel signs are *never* written to it. When a vowel occurs before *s* initially, the stroke *s* must be used ; thus,

sap, *spa*, *asp*, *sack*, *ask*.

Similarly, when a vowel occurs after *s* or *z* finally, **the** stroke must be used ; thus,

daze, *daisy*, *gas*, *gassy*.

Exercise 6

Read, copy, and transcribe

1.

2.

3.

4. [shorthand outlines]

5. [shorthand outlines]

6. [shorthand outlines]

Exercise 7

Write in Shorthand

1. Picks, bakes, baits, fades, feeds, paths, fix, dates.
2. Tapes, takes, stay, stays, tips, pitches, seat, seats.
3. Days, sacks, gas, pass, peeks, these, attacks, acid.
4. Bees, busy, daze, daisy, dishes, cedes, debts, pities.
5. Cask, disc, tasks, desks, visits, basic, sixth, evasive.
6. Besieges, beseech, passage, passages, visage, deceive, deceives.

GRAMMALOGS

[shorthand] had, [shorthand] do, [shorthand] different or difference ; [shorthand] much, [shorthand] which ; [shorthand] large ; [shorthand] can, [shorthand] come ; [shorthand] go, [shorthand] give or given ; [shorthand] for ; [shorthand] have ; [shorthand] thank or thanked, [shorthand] think ; [shorthand] as or has, [shorthand] is or his.

Exercise 8

Read, copy, and transcribe

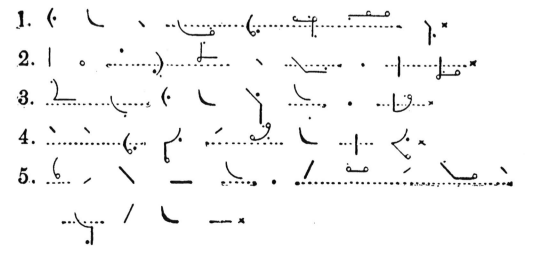

Exercise 9

Write in Shorthand

1. *Who can go to the* safe *and* get *all of the* checks ?
2. *Do* they *think the* desks *too large for* these passages ?
3. They said *his* speeches *ought to be given on different* days.
4. If Debbs keeps faith, *all of* these debts *of his can be* paid.
5. *It* keeps Bates busy *to* visit *all of the* ships *which come to the* city.

SUMMARY

1. The consonant *sh* may be written either upward or downward, whichever makes the easier joining.

2. Circle *s* is read first at the beginning of an outline and last at the end.

3. The small circle may represent either *s* or *z* in the middle or at the end of an outline.

4. Vowel-signs are always written alongside a stroke, never to a circle.

LESSON III

12. The Remainder of the Consonants. The last eight consonants do not occur in pairs, but *r* and *h* are each provided with two signs, making ten signs altogether ; thus,

Letter	Character	Name	As sounded in	
M	⌢	em	met	seem
N	⌣	en	net	seen
NG	⌣	ing	kingly	long
L	(up	el	light	tile
R	down / up	ar, ray	tire	right
W	⤹ up	way	wet	away
Y	⤸ up	yay	yet	Yale
H	⟋ down ⟋ up	hay	high	adhere

For convenience the upstroke for *r* is called *ray*. The signs for *m*, *n*, *ng*, are written from left to right, and *w* and *y* are upstrokes. The signs for *h* begin in each case at the circle end ; thus ⟋ (up), ⟋ (down). The consonant (*l* is always written upward when standing alone.

Position Writing. The first downstroke or upstroke in the outline indicates its position ; thus,

⟋ *agency*, ⌢ *lame*, ⟍ *racks*, ⟋ *kills*.

13

Exercise 10

Read, copy and transcribe

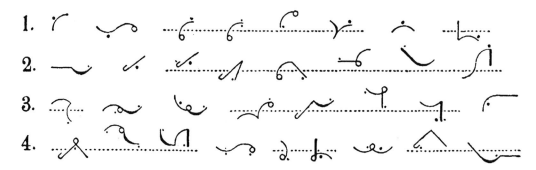

Write in Shorthand

5. May, make, makes, scene, scenes, ill, sale, sales.
6. Sills, lease, weigh, weighs, yes, mail, mails, shells.
7. Mills, sells, leaps, leads, slap, slaps, many, niece.
8. Weep, weeps, weeds, bank, banks, scheme, schemes.
9. Navy, miss, missive, web, misty, escapes, excel, shale.

13. **The Use of the Alternative Forms. L Written Downward.** The consonant ⌠ *l* may be written either upward or downward with equal ease. Thus after *n* or *ng* it is usually written downward because a sharper and more convenient angle is formed as—

⌐ *kneel,* ⌐ *nails,* ⌐ *seemingly.*

Similarly when ⌠ *l* precedes a circle and curve, or follows a curve and circle, it is written in the same direction as the circle, as—

⌐ *listen,* ⌐ *lesser,* ⌐ *Neilsen,* ⌐ *nasal,* ⌐ *measles.*

Exercise 11

Write in Shorthand

1. Lily, delay, lacing, kingly, kill, canal, bale.
2. Vessel, cancel, nestle, leak, namely, lease, leasing.

Upward and Downward R. (*a*) The object of having alternative signs for *r* is to indicate the presence or absence of a vowel-sound. In words beginning with a vowel followed by *r*, or ending with the sound of *r*, the downward form is used, as—

＼ *air*, ＼ *fair*, ◯ *ear*, ⌐ *tear*.

On the other hand, if the word begins with *r*, or ends with *r* and a sounded vowel, then the upward form is used, as—

△ *wrap*, ◡ *ring*, ∨ *berry*, ∨ *ferry*.

(*b*) When initial *r* is immediately followed by *m*, the downward *r* is written because of the greater ease in joining ; thus,

◯ *ream*, ◯ *rim*, ◯ *arm*.

(*c*) Write the *r* either upward or downward, regardless of vowels, to avoid an awkward joining. Thus, before *t*, *d*, *ch*, *j*, *th* or *TH*, upward *r* makes a faster and easier joining, as—

⊿ *arid*, ⊿ *arch*, ⋋ *earth*.

Likewise, after ＼, ＼, ◡ or the single straight up-strokes ╱, ╱, ╱, ╱, upward *r* is used for the same reason, as—

⌐ *defacer*, ◡ *Vassar*, ◡ *answer*, ╱ *rear*, ╱ *racer*, ◡ *aware*.

(*d*) In words like *fare* the vowel-sound is represented by the second-place heavy dot ; thus,

⌐ *dare*, ⌐ *tear*, ＼ *pair*.

Exercise 12
Write in Shorthand

1. Read, ready, err, airily, risk, risks, receive, par.
2. Raise, racing, Irving, rag, pair, rare, jeer, share.
3. Marry, car, carry, answer, remiss, raid, arrayed.

Upward and Downward H. The downward form of *h* is used when that consonant stands alone, or when it **is** immediately followed by ___ or ___, as—

     hay,   *hake,*   *Hague,*   *hags.*

Otherwise, as a general rule, it is better to employ the upward form of *h*.

Exercise 13

Read, copy, and transcribe

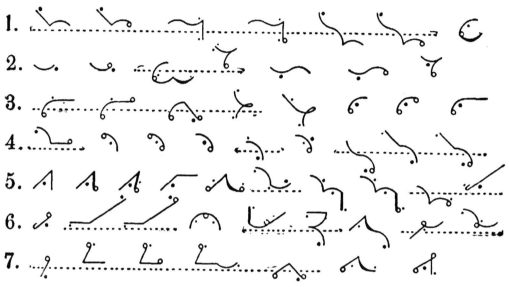

Write in Shorthand

8. Tame, tames, dames, James, games, maims, snakes.
9. Pale, pales, bales, tales, males, deals, snails, lacings.
10. Shame, shames, shell, vessels, nasal, missile, manly.
11. Ram, rams, array, sheer, Arab, cherry, answers.
12. Nave, naves, sneeze, revenge, reddish, lavish, fishing.
13. Wade, wades, yea, basin, receipt, receipts, salary.
14. Head, heads, hedge, hedges, hitch, hitches, business.

GRAMMALOGS

(*though,* (*them ;*) *was,* ___ *whose ;* ⌡ *shall,* ___ *wish ;*

⌡ *usual-ly ;* ⌒ *me,* ⌒ *him ;* ⌣ *in* or *any,* ___ *own ;*

⌣ *language* or *owing,* ⌣ *thing,* ___ *young ;* ⟍ *your,*

⟍ *year ;* ╱ *we.*

Exercise 14

Read, copy, and transcribe

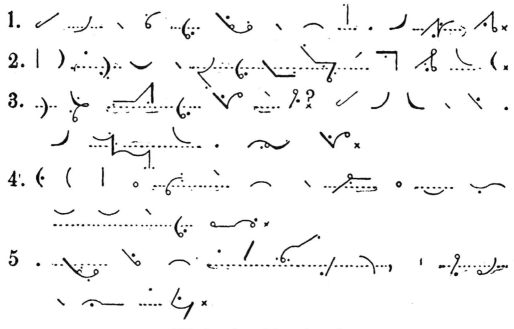

Write in Shorthand

6. *We shall* ask *him to give his* speech *in a different language to*-day.

7. *All the* dealers *in your* vicinity seem *to think* they *can* manage *the* affair easily.

8. *Though* he *has* many enemies, *all of them* seem *to be* aware *of his* mental agility *and* business ability.

9. *The* head *of the* firm *thinks it was a* rash *thing for the young* cashier *to do.* *It* may affect *his* career.

10. If *we* appeal *to* James Nelsen he may *give me all the* facts *in the* legacy case.

SUMMARY

1. The consonants *r* and *h* have alternative forms.

2. When standing alone *l* is written upward.

3. Stroke *l* preceding a circle and curve or following a curve and circle is written in the direction of the circle.

4. Use *r* initially if a vowel precedes. Use *ray* finally if a vowel follows.

2—(445) *Can.*

LESSON IV

14. **The Dash Vowels.** A heavy dash, in the first, second, and third-place respectively, represents the long vowels *aw*, *ō*, *o͞o*, as heard in the words *bought, boat,* and *boot.* A light dash, similarly, represents the corresponding short vowels *ŏ*, *ŭ*, *o͝o*, as heard in the words *hot, hut,* and *hood;* thus,

FIRST-PLACE DASH VOWELS—

aw, and the corresponding short *ŏ*, occupy first place, as

⟍ *bought,* ⌐ *chalk,* ⌐ *law,* ⌐ *top,* ⌐ *lodge,* ⟍ *rock.*

SECOND-PLACE DASH VOWELS—

ō, and the corresponding short *ŭ*, occupy second place, as

⟍ *vote,* ⟍ *cope,* ⟍ *fore,* ⌐ *tub,* ⟋ *rug,* ⟍ *love.*

THIRD-PLACE DASH VOWELS—

o͞o, and the corresponding short *o͝o*, occupy third place, as

⟍ *boot,* ⟋ *cool,* ⌐ *loom,* ⟍ *pull,* ⟍ *bull,* ⟍ *book.*

(*a*) In words like *fore* the vowel sound is represented by the second-place heavy dash ; thus,

⌐ *door,* ⌐ *tore,* ⟍ *pour.*

Exercise 15

Read, copy, and transcribe

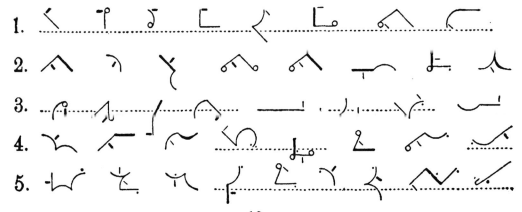

18

Write in Shorthand

6. Ball, balk, lauds, hawks, dots, knobs, mocks, song.
7. Votes, boats, scope, hoax, does, dusty, luck, cups.
8. Spools, food, poor, rooms, took, looks, hooks, hood.
9. Hurry, hero, loosen, losing, muscle, roar, locked, bore.
10. Sung, shawl, shawls, urge, officer, dozen, wrongly,

15. Loops for St and Str. A small loop represents *st*, and a larger loop represents *str*. These loops are written, like circle *s*, inside of curves, and with a left motion to straight strokes ; thus,

pass, past, pastor, pastors ;

mass, mast, master, masters ;

soup, stoop, stoops ;

seed, steed ; seal, steal.

(*a*) Following a *st* or a *str* loop, the circle *s* is written as indicated in the words *pastors* and *masters*.

(*b*) The *st* loop is written at the beginning or end of a stroke. The *str* loop *is never written at the beginning of a stroke.* Both the *st* and *str* loops may be used medially ; thus,

toasting, masterpiece, lastingly.

(*c*) Just as the small circle at the end of a stroke may represent *s* or *z*, so the small loop at the end of a stroke may represent *st* or *zd*, as in

suppose, supposed.

(*d*) The *st* loop cannot be employed when a vowel occurs between *s* and *t* because there must be a stroke consonant to provide a place for the vowel-sign. Compare—

best, beset ; rest, receipt.

For the same reason the *str* loop may not be written when a strongly sounded vowel occurs between *st* and *r.* Compare—

꜡ *rooster,*   ꜡ *restore.*

The *st* loop cannot be employed finally when a vowel follows *t* ; thus,

꜡ *best,*   ꜡ *bestow ;*   ꜡ *rest,*   ꜡ *rusty.*

Exercise 16

Read, copy, and transcribe

1.
2.
3.
4.

Write in Shorthand

5. Steps, stems, disposed, fullest, steal, tacit, just, discussed.
6. Forests, list, enlisting, dismissed, assists, rests, arrests, Saturday.
7. Musters, ministers, lustre, investors, waster, register, pester.
8. Adjust, adjusting, adjuster, dusting, jesting, bolster, exits, smoothest.

16. **The Halving Principle.** Light strokes are halved to indicate the addition of *t*, and heavy strokes to indicate the addition of *d* ; thus,

꜡ *pay,* ꜡ *pate,* ꜡ *paid ;* ꜡ *tap,* ꜡ *tapped ;* ꜡ *web,* ꜡ *webbed ;* ꜡ *lift,* ꜡ *lived ;* ꜡ *fat,* ꜡ *feed.*

The *d* in many words is pronounced *t*, as in *tapped* (tapt).

(*a*) In words of more than one syllable, a stroke may be halved for either *t* or *d* ; thus,

⟋ *pity*, ⟍ *pitied* ; ⟍ *vote*, ⟍ *voted* ; ⟍ *orb*, ⟍ *orbit* ; ⟍ *rapid*, ⟍ *rabbit* ; ⟍ *note*, ⟍ *noted* ; ⟍ *evidence*.

(*b*) A final *s* circle attached to a half-length stroke is read after the *t* or *d* ; thus,

⟋ *repeats*, ⟍ *invades*.

(*c*) If a vowel sound occurs after a final *t* or *d*, a full-length stroke must be used ; thus,

⟋ *chatty*, ⟍ *body*.

17. Omission of Obscure Vowels. An obscure or unaccented vowel in the middle of a word may be omitted ; thus,

⟍ *answer*, ⟍ *answered* ; ⟍ *officer*, ⟍ *officered* ; ⟋ *relay*, ⟋ *relate*, ⟋ *relates*, ⟋ *related*

Exercise 17

Read, copy, and transcribe

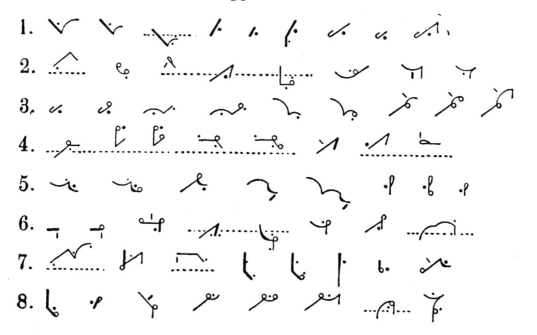

GRAMMALOGS

╱ *are*, ⟋ *our* or *hour* ; ⟨ *that*, ⟨ *without* ; ～ *sent* ;

▭ *quite*, ▁ *could* ; ⌒ *most* ; ⌣ *influence*, ⌣ *influenced*,

⌣ *next* ; ○ *first* ; ⌒ *myself*, ⌒ *himself*.

Exercise 18

Read, copy, and transcribe

1.

2.

3.

4.

5.

6.

7.

8.

9.

Exercise 19

Write in Shorthand

(Note that *caused* is written ⊓ to distinguish
the word from ▭ *cost*.)

1. See *to it that the two* deeds *are sent to* Messrs. Stanley
and Foster *in different* envelopes.
2. *The* note they *sent* us states *that* they *have* disposed *of*
most of the stock *in* Toronto *and* Ottawa.

3. *Our* " Star Dusters " *are* selling rapidly *in the* city *of* Nelson. *We could* not make *them quite* fast enough.

4. James Dexter's *much* discussed stories appear *in the* " Saturday Post." Read *them*.

5. *It was the* low cost *of* these silk waists *that* caused *the* rush *for them* at *the* sale.

6. *We* hope they *have* succeeded *in* leasing *for* us *the* stores *we* wanted *in* Moose Jaw.

7. Thomas Baxter *has* wasted *much* money *in his* business deals *and has* only *himself to thank for his* heavy loss.

8. *We* noticed *that the* " Cadillac Roadster " *was the* car *most in* evidence at *the* recent automobile show.

SUMMARY

1. When occurring between two strokes, dash vowels follow the rules given for the dot vowels.

2. A small loop represents *st* and a large loop *str*.

3. The *str* loop is not used initially.

4. The sign for an obscure vowel may be omitted.

5. Light strokes are halved for *t*, heavy strokes for *d* ; but in words of more than one syllable a stroke may be halved for either *t* or *d*.

6. Read the *s* circle last when it is attached finally to a half-length stroke.

LESSON V

18. Large Circles for Sw and Ss. A large circle *at the beginning* of a stroke represents *sw*, and, like the small circle *s*, is written with the left motion to a straight stroke and inside a curve ; thus,

soup, *swoop* ; *soon*, *swoon*.

(*a*) A large circle written *in the middle* of a word *or at the end* of a stroke represents the light or heavy sound of two *s*'s, with an intervening vowel. It is also written with the left motion to a straight stroke and inside a curve. When a vowel other than *ĕ* intervenes, it is indicated by placing the vowel-sign within the circle ; thus,

pass, *passes* ; *doze*, *dozes* ; *mass*, *masses*, *miss*, *misses*, *Mississippi* ; *raise*, *raises*, *resist* ; *sense*, *senses*, *census* ; *success*, *successes*.

(*b*) As in the case of the *st* and *str* loops, final circle *s* following the large circle is written as indicated in the word *successes*.

Exercise 20

Read, copy, and transcribe

1.
2.
3.
4.
5.
6.

Write in Shorthand

7. Seat, sweet, sweetest, seed, Swede, Swedish, sweep, swept, switched.

8. Swift, swiftest, suave, swath, swimmer, swells, swore, swings.

9. Oppose, opposes, disposes, debases, notices, chooses, juices, success, resources.

10. Emphasis, ceases, amazes, evinces, releases, thesis, purses, Colossus.

11. Exist, existed, Texas, successor, insist, insists, insisted.

12. Resisted, exhaust, exhausted, synopsis, necessity, necessitates, accessory.

19. Tick and Dot H. The downstroke *h* is contracted to a mere tick before the strokes ⌢ ⌒ ⟍ , as in—

⌁ *home*, ⌁ *hail*, ⟍ *hair*.

This tick *h* is used only initially, as in the examples just given. If stroke *h*, either upward or downward, should be awkward to write in the middle of a word, the sound of *h* is expressed by a light dot placed before the vowel-sign ; thus,

⌁ *unhandy*, ⌁ *mishap*, ⟍ *uphill*, ⌁ *loophole*.

The dot *h* is merely an alternative to the stroke form of *h*, and should be used only when the stroke form is inconvenient.

Exercise 21

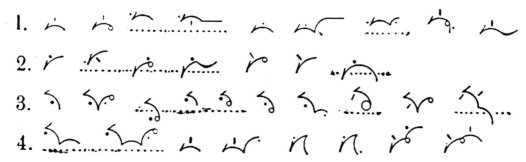

5. [shorthand outlines]

6. [shorthand outlines]

7. [shorthand outlines]

GRAMMALOGS AND CONTRACTIONS

⌐ *because*, ⌐ *itself*; ⌐ *those*, ⌐ *this*, ⌐ *thus*; ⌐ *several*,

⌐ *themselves*, ⌐ *ourselves*, ⌐ *influences*; ⌐ *anything*,

⌐ *something*, ⌐ *nothing*; ⌐ *as is*, ⌐ *is as*.

Exercise 22

Read, copy, and transcribe

1. [shorthand outlines]

2. [shorthand outlines]

3. [shorthand outlines]

4. [shorthand outlines]

5. [shorthand outlines]

6. [shorthand outlines]

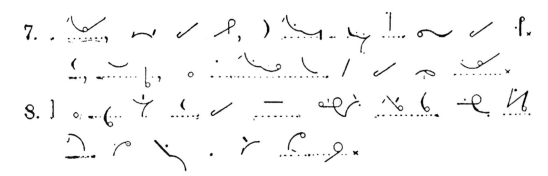

Exercise 23

Write in Shorthand

1. *Without your influence and* help, *our* appeals *to the* state officers *are of* no use.

2. *It* appears *that several of the* leading firms *in this* city *are* seeking *a* monopoly *of the* wholesale tobacco business.

3. Recent statistics show *that the* cost *of* living necessities *has* changed *but* little *in the* past *two years.*

Messrs. Sweeney *&* Swift,

    Rochester, Minnesota.

Sirs :

 The boxes *of* Swiss laces reached us *on* Wednesday, *but because of the* long *and* unnecessary delay *we have* lost *two* good customers. *Several of the* smaller lace hangings *are of the* wrong shape *and we shall* ship *them* back *to the* wholesale dealers. These successive errors *have* caused us many needless risks *of* losing some *of our* best customers. *We* insist *that* changes *in your* business policy *are* certainly needed if *we are to* make *a* success *of it* here.

       Yours,

SUMMARY

1. A large initial circle represents *sw.*

2. A large medial or final circle represents *ss* or *sz.*

3. The tick *h* is prefixed to   ⌢ ⌢ ⌝

4. The dot *h* is used as an alternative to the stroke *h,* when the latter cannot be easily written.

LESSON VI

20. Diphthongs. The sounds $\bar{\imath}$, ow, oi, $\bar{u}$, heard in the sentence *I now enjoy music*, are called diphthongs, because each consists of two vowels combined into one sound. The sign for the diphthong $\bar{\imath}$ is the lower half of a diamond, thus, ∨ ; the sign for the diphthong ow is the upper half of a diamond, thus, ∧ The sign for oi is a small ▁ (*k*) and / (*ch*) joined together, thus, ⊐ ; and the sign for $\bar{u}$ is the upper half of a small circle, thus, ⌒ The signs for $\bar{\imath}$ and oi are written in the first vowel-place, as in—

$\searrow$ *pie*, $\searrow$ *spy*, $\searrow$ *boy*, $\lceil$ *toy ;*

the signs for ow and $\bar{u}$ are written in the third vowel-place, as in—

loud, *rout*, *cow*. *cube*, *duke*, *duty*.

21. Joined Diphthongs. Diphthongs are joined initially and finally to stroke consonants wherever it can be done easily. To make an easy joining, the semicircle for $\bar{u}$ may be written sideways, thus, $\smile$ *value*, $\smile$ *new ;* and the sign for ow abbreviated, thus, $\smile$ *now*. When preceding *k, g, m,* or upward *l,* the diphthong $\bar{\imath}$ is contracted, as in $\surd$ *isle* or *I'll.*

(*a*) The vowel *aw* may be joined to upward *l,* as in *also*.

(*b*) The sign for *all* is used in words like *already,* *always.*

(*c*) Where a final diphthong is joined, the stroke consonant may be halved for *t* or *d,* as in ⅄ *doubt,* $\smile$ *feud.*

28

Exercise 24

Read, copy, and transcribe

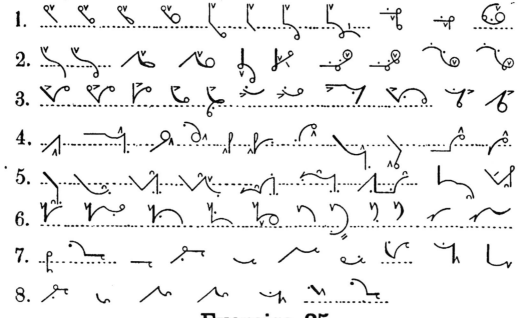

Exercise 25

Write in Shorthand

1. Timely, piracy, verify, admire, writhe, retires, satisfy, satisfied, hires.
2. Analyze, analyzes, reviser, wide, widely, wisely, rises, arises, sometimes.
3. Enjoy, enjoyed, rejoiced, spoiling, invoices, noises, toys, soil.
4. Refuge, rebuke, assumes, duties, hugely, cures, occupied, refusal, excuses.
5. Announce, announces, announced, loudest, loudly, mouths, boughs.
6. Ensue, retinue, mute, night, cute, ivy, aisle, bowed, revenue.

22. **Triphones.** The vowel which follows a diphthong in very many words is expressed by a light tick, joined to the diphthong and written so as to make a sharp angle with it ; thus,

dial, manual, Iowa.

The sign representing a diphthong and a vowel is called a *triphone*, because it expresses three vowels in one sign.

23. Abbreviated W. A small right semicircle is prefixed to __ *k*, __ *g*, ⌒ *m*, ＼ *r* and ╱ *ray*, to represent the initial sound of *w*, thus,

⊥ *walk*, ⌒ *wake*, ⌒ *womanly*, ＼ *wore*, ╱ *worry*.

The semicircle is *always read first*, so that if a word begins with a vowel the stroke ╱ *w* must be used. Compare ⌒ *wake*, ╱ *awake*; ＼ *ware*, ╱ *aware*.

Exercise 26

Read, copy, and transcribe

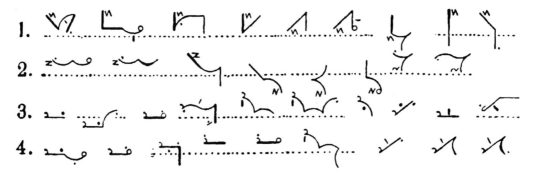

Exercise 27

Write in Shorthand

1. Fiery, dial, via, pioneer, bias, violence, violate, violated.
2. Voyage, loyal, loyalty, moiety, cower, cowers, bower, endower.
3. Genuine, eventually, duel, fewer, suicide, insinuate, reviewer.
4. Walk, walked, walker, worried, were, weary, aware, wars, warlike, war-time.

24. Phrasing. Two or more shorthand outlines may be written together whenever an easy joining can be made. This practice is a great help in developing speed, and the student should, therefore, cultivate the ability to write phrases easily.

The first word in a phrase must occupy the position which it would occupy if it stood alone.

I, I've (= I have), I'm (= I am),

I'll (= I will), I will be;

you, you may, you will, you will be,

you should be.

A first-place sign may be slightly raised or lowered, however, to accommodate the following stroke, as

I thank you, I think you should, I have,

I view, I had, I do.

25. Tick *the*. A small tick attached finally and written in the direction of *ray* or *chay*, indicates the word *the*; thus,

I have the, at the, to the, by the,

on the (slightly turned to distinguish from I).

Practice the following phrases until they can be written with ease. Phrases, as a rule, need not be vocalized, but a vowel may be inserted where necessary, as

I may, to distinguish from I am.

I will		If you will
I will be		if you will be
I will do		if you are
I can		if you should
I am		if you should be
I may		if you should know
I may be		we have
I have		we have seen
I have seen		we know
I have no		we think
I have such		we think you should
I have just		we think you should be
I have it		they will
I think		they will be
I think you should		it will be
I think you may		it may be
you will		you were
you will be		if you were
you will do		which were
you will have		they were
you should		we were
you should be		

Note that in phrases the stroke ⌒ is used for *will* and the stroke ⌍ for *were*. When the ⌍ does not join easily, the strokes ⟋ are used instead.

GRAMMALOGS AND CONTRACTIONS

∧ *how;* ⌐ *why;* ⌐ *with,* ⌐ *when;* ⌐ *what,* ⌐ *would;*
⌐ *beyond,* ⌐ *you;* ⌐ *knowledge,* ⌐ *acknowledge,*
⌐ *acknowledged;* ⌐ *O, Oh, owe,* ⌐ *he.*

PHRASES

⌐ *New York;* ⌐ *United States.*

(When *he* stands alone, or is the first word in a phrase, the form ⌐ is employed. In all other cases the sign ⌐ is written.)

Exercise 28

Read, copy, and transcribe

Exercise 29

Write in Shorthand

In the following type exercises throughout this book, the use of a hyphen between words indicates that they should be phrased.

1. *Although* I-*have* argued *with him and* emphasized-*the* value *of a* worthy career, I doubt if I-*can influence his* choice.

2. *It-is a* little early *to-think* about-*the* annual exhibit now, *but we-shall* discuss *it with you when you* arrive *in* New-York.

3. *What you have* asked us *to-do is beyond our* power. *We-can* help *you* only if-*you* renew *all your* licenses annually.

4. *The* pieces *of* china-ware *which*-were *on* sale were *all* sold out by-*the* time I reached *the* store.

5. *The* heavy smoke *that* obscures *your* view *is* caused by-*the* soft coal now used so widely.

6. *We* rejoice *to* hear *that-you have* invited *the* famous singer *to* appear *in a* series *of* recitals *in-the* United-States *and-that-he-has* accepted.

7. *How-can-we* elect *a* new set *of* officers *for our* society *when those* now *in* power refuse *to*-resign ?

Exercise 30

Read, copy, and transcribe

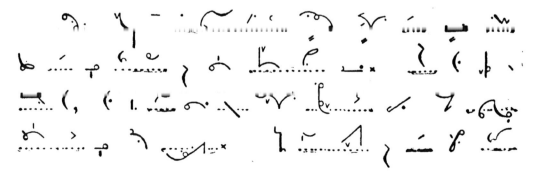

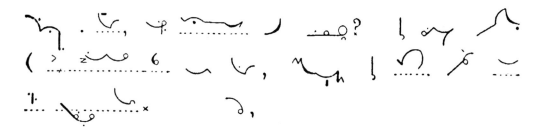

SUMMARY

1. The diphthongs *ī* and *oi* are written in the first-place, and *ow* and *ū* in the third-place.

2. Diphthongs may be joined when convenient.

3. A vowel following a diphthong is expressed by **a** light tick joined to the diphthong.

4. The first word of a phrase must be written in its own position, and in phrasing a light tick represents *the*.

5. A stroke with a finally-joined diphthong may be halved for either *t* or *d*.

6. A small right semicircle is prefixed to the strokes — — ⌒ ⟍ ⟋ to represent the sound of *w*.

LESSON VII

26. Circle and Stroke S and the Loops St and Str. A vowel-sign is never written to a circle or a loop. Therefore, a stroke consonant must always be written whenever it is necessary to indicate the presence of a vowel sound. The following illustrations show that the vowel-sign is written in each case, not to a circle or loop, but to a stroke. Note also that when a word begins with *z*, the stroke) is employed.

(*a*)) *ace,*) *aces ;*) *ice,*) *ices ;*) *sigh,*) *sighs,*) *assize ;* ⌒ *am,* ⌒ *Sam,* ⌐ *Assam ;* │ *add,* │ *sad,*) *acid ;* ⌐ *ale,* ⌐ *sale,* ⌐ *assail ;* ⟍ *pie,* ⟍ *spy,*) *espy ;*) *sue,*) *sues,*) *suicide ;*) *see,*) *sees,*) *Caesar ;* ⌒ *sense,*) *essence,*) *zoo,*) *zeal,*) *Zulu.*

(*b*) ⟍ *bees,* ⟍ *busy ;* ⌒ *noise,* ⌐ *noisy ;* ⟋ *rose,* ⟍ *rosy ;* ⌐ *less,* ⌐ *lessee.*

(*c*) ⟍ *paste,* ⟍ *pasty,* ⟍ *pastime ;* ⟍ *best,* ⟍ *bestow,* ⟍ *beset ;* ⟋ *rust,* ⟍ *rusty,* ⟍ *russet ;* ⟍ *past,* ⟍ *pastor,* ⟍ *pasture ;* ⟍ *vest,* ⟍ *vestor,* ⟍ *vesture ;* ⌒ *monster,* ⌒ *monastery.*

27. Stroke S in Compound Words. The stroke *s* is retained in derivatives and compounds formed from words in which *s* or *z* is the only consonant sound, as in *sea, saw, ace, ice, ease ;* thus,

$\int$ *saw,* $\check{\int}($ *sawmill ;*).. *sea,*)... *sea-coast,*

).. *ease,* $\searrow$: *easily.*

The stroke *s* is also written—

(*a*) When a triphone immediately follows initial *s ;* thus,

∞ *sense,* $\mathcal{L}_\circ$ *science,* $\widehat{}$ *Syme,* $\mathcal{L}$ *Siam.*

(*b*) When the syllable *-ous* is immediately preceded by a diphthong, as in

$\searrow$) *pious,* $\int^z$ *joyous,* $\underline{\sim}$) *sinuous.*

28. **Vowel Indication.** The preceding explanations show that in very many cases it is possible to indicate an initial or a final vowel without using the vowel-sign. Thus, in words like $\underline{\quad}$ *aside,* $\underline{}$ *ask,* $\searrow$ *asleep,* the use of the stroke *s* at the beginning indicates a preceding vowel. If the words were *side, sack, sleep,* the outlines would be $\underline{\int}$ *side,* $\underline{}$ *sack,* $\bigwedge$ *sleep.* Similarly, in words like $\underline{\neg}$ *misty,* $\bigvee\!\!\big)$ *policy,* $\big/\!\!\big)$ *jealousy,* the use of a stroke for the last consonant indicates a following vowel. If the words were *mist, police, jealous,* the outlines would be $\frown$ *mist,* $\bigvee$: *police,* $\big/$° *jealous.*

(*a*) In the same way a downward *r* initially almost always suggests a preceding vowel, as in $\underline{\smallfrown}$ *argue,* $\searrow$ *arisen ;* while the use of an upward *r* finally, as in $\diagup$ *marry,* $\underline{\diagup}$ *carry,* indicates a following vowel. Note the difference in outline between $\underline{\smallfrown}$ *argue* and $\diagup$ *rag,* $\searrow$ *arisen* and $\underline{\smallsmile}$ *risen,* $\diagup$ *marry* and $\frown$ *mar,* and $\underline{\diagup}$ *carry* and $\underline{\diagdown}$ *car.*

(*b*) When an initial *l* immediately precedes a simple horizontal stroke, it is written downward if the word begins with a vowel and upward if the first sound is *l* ; thus,

⟋ *alike*,   ⟋ *elm*,   ⟋ *alone*,   ⟍ *along*,

but ⟋ *like*,   ⌒ *lame*,   ⌒ *Luna*,   ⌒ *long*.

(*c*) Similarly, when final *l* follows ⟍ ⟍ ⟋ or any straight upstroke, the upward form is used to indicate a following vowel, and the downward form to indicate the absence of a vowel ; thus,

⟍ *fell*, but ⟍ *fellow*;   ⟍ *vale*, but ⟍ *valley*;

⟋ *scale*, but ⟋ *scaly*;   ⟋ *rail*, but ⟋ *rely*.

(*d*) In words like ⟍ *debar* and ⟍ *Shakespeare*,

where *r* follows two downstrokes, the upward *r* is written, so as to keep the outline close to the line of writing ; and for the same reason the downward *r* is used finally after two straight upstrokes, as in ⟍ *rarer*.

Exercise 31

Read, copy, and transcribe

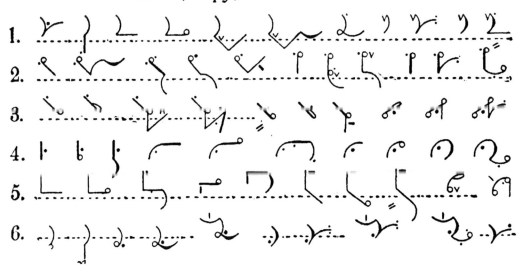

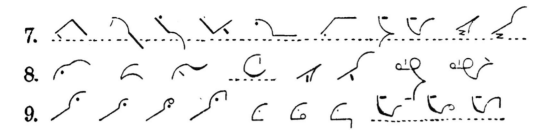

Exercise 32

Write in Shorthand

1. Sleep, asleep, slope, aslope, state, estate, asylum.
2. Skip, escape, said, essayed, seek, Eskimo, sum, assume.
3. Pose, posy, bees, busy, case, Casey, rest, receipt.
4. Dust, dusty, deceit, arid, aright, earth, arch, urges.
5. Far, ferry, appear, parry, boor, bureau, jeer, jury.
6. Full, fully, veal, villa, skill, sickly, yell, yellow.
7. Elk, leak, Olga, log, alum, lime, facile, vessels, swiftly.
8. License, licensed, unlicensed, assail, assault, assaults.
9. Despair, bestir, disperses, disposer, posture, roarer.

GRAMMALOGS AND CONTRACTIONS

↘ *special* or *specially,* ↘ *speak;* ⌐ *dollar,* ⌐ *dollars;*

↘ *establish-ed-ment;* ↘ *expect-ed;* ↘ *unexpected;*

⎓ *altogether,* ⌐ *together;* ↗ *insurance;* ↙ *January;*

↘ *February;* ↘ *November* or *never;* ⌐ *yesterday;*

↗ *regular,* ↘ *irregular.*

Exercise 33

Read, copy, and transcribe

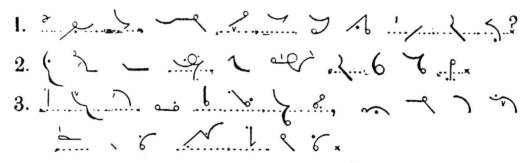

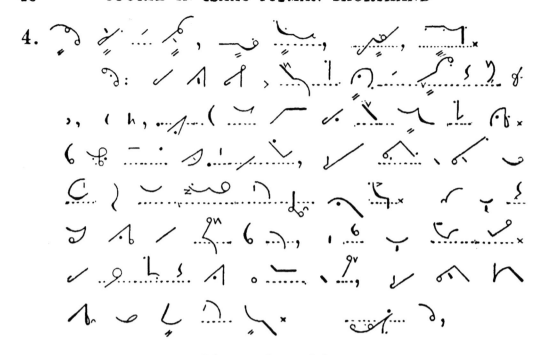

Exercise 34

Write in Shorthand

1. *We-have* notified *him that-he-is to speak to-*morrow night *on-the* bonus.

2. *Our* officers despair *of-his* ability or desire *to* change *his irregular* methods *and* habits.

3. *The regular* notices *of-the* society *are sent to-him* also, yet he-*has never* received *any of-them*.

4. Robson & Scholes, Ottawa, Canada.

   Sirs :

   We-are exceedingly sorry *to* hear *that-you* do not like-*the* pastes *we-sent several* days ago. *We* suggest *that-*they *be sent* back *to* us, *and-we-shall* ship new tubes *to-you without* delay. *We* desire *to* emphasize *our* policy *of a* " thoroughly satisfied customer, or no sale." *Our* success testifies *to-the* wisdom *of-*such *a* policy.

   We hope *you-*will not hesitate *to-*let us know if-*the* new lot *is* not up *to-the* mark, *as-it-is* only *thus that-the* firm *and its* customers *can* satisfy *themselves*.

   Yours,

SUMMARY

1. An initial vowel requires the use of an initial stroke, and a final vowel requires the use of a final stroke.

2. The stroke *s* is written in derivatives and compounds, when a triphone immediately follows initial *s*, and in the syllable *-ous* when this is preceded by a diphthong.

3. The use of the upward and downward forms of *r* and *l* enables the writer to indicate, in many words, the presence or absence of an initial or a final vowel.

LESSON VIII

29. Initial Hook for L to Straight Strokes. A small initial hook written with the left motion adds *l* to the straight strokes *p, b, t, d, ch, j, k* and *g* ; thus,

⟍ *pl,* ⟍ *bl,* Ⅰ *tl,* Ⅰ *dl,* ⌐ *ch l,* ⌐ *jl,* ⌐ *kl,* ⌐ *gl.*

(*a*) These double consonants are vocalized and read like single consonants. The circle *s* is prefixed to them by writing the circle inside the initial hook. The illustrations which follow show also how to join this hook in the middle of a word—

⟍ *pie,* ⟍ *ply,* ⟍ *supply,* ⌐⟍ *imply ;* ⟍ *able,*

⟍ *sable,* ⌐ *table ;* Ⅰ *set,* Ⅰ *settle,* ⟍ *battle ;* Ⅰ *addle,*

Ⅰ *saddle,* ⟍ *paddle ;* Ⅰ *satchel,* ⟍ *chapel ;* ⅂ *cudgel ;*

⌐ *clay,* ⌐ *cycle,* Ⅰ *tickle ;* ⌐ *eagle,* ⌐ *Siegel.*

⟍ *bugle.*

Exercise 35

Read, copy, and transcribe

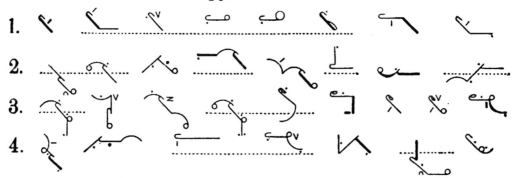

Write in Shorthand

5. Play, plate, plates, places, plasters, replies, replied.
6. Foibles, cables, enabled, bottles, pliable, bluster, black.
7. Close, closes, claims, clasp, glass, glasses, globe, glory.
8. Deplore, label, inclose, inclosed, smuggle, smuggled.
9. Sublime, secluded, subtle, supplied, settled, settlers.

30. Initial Hook for R to Straight Strokes. A small initial hook written with the right motion adds *r* to the straight strokes *p, b, t, d, ch, j, k* and *g* ; thus,

$\diagdown$ *pr,* $\diagdown$ *br,* $\rceil$ *tr,* $\rceil$ *dr,* $\diagup$ *ch r,* $\diagup$ *jr,* $-$ *kr,* $\frown$ *gr.*

(*a*) These double consonants also are vocalized and read like single consonants.

A circle or loop may be prefixed to these double consonants by writing the circle or loop on the same side as the hook *r.* The hook is used medially also ; thus,

$\diagdown$ *pray,* $\diagdown$ *spray,* $\diagdown$ *paper ;* $\diagdown$ *bray,* $\diagdown$ *sabre,* $\diagdown$ *fibre ;* $\dashv$ *eater,* $\dashv$ *sweeter,* $\diagdown$ *better,* $\dashv$ *outer,* $\dashv$ *stouter ;* $\dashv$ *eider,* $\dashv$ *cider,* $\diagdown$ *louder ;* $\diagup$ *etcher,* $\diagdown$ *stretcher,* $\diagdown$ *preacher ;* $\diagup$ *edger,* $\diagup$ *stager,* $\diagdown$ *ledger ;* $\dashv$ *ochre,* $\dashv$ *soaker,* $\dashv$ *stoker,* $\frown$ *maker.*

The hooked forms may represent syllables in words like—

$\diagdown$ *terminus,* $\diagdown$ *delicacy,* $\diagdown$ *perplex.*

Exercise 36

Read, copy, and transcribe

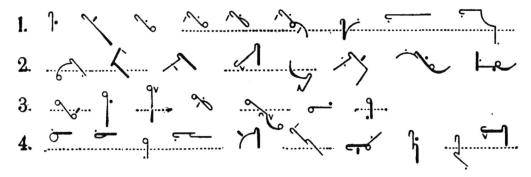

Write in Shorthand

5. Praises, praised, bruise, bruised, address, addresses, addressed, gray, graze.

6. Labor, teacher, major, depressed, packers, bigger, imprison, biography.

7. Sweeper, supreme, steeper, sober, utter, stutter, sweater, sicker, stickers.

8. Stress, stresses, presently, trials, grazes, cruiser, grasps, streams, strong.

9. Strike, strikers, brighter, progress, struggles, troubles, brutal, grapple, glitters.

31. **Medial Circle and Hook.** When a circle and a hook are used medially, both circle and hook must be shown ; thus,

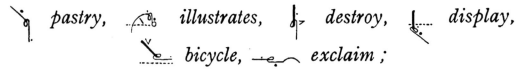

but when an easy joining is not possible, the *l* hook is not used medially ; thus,

pistol, unsettle, accessible.

(*a*) When *skr* or *sgr* follows *t* or *d*, the combinations are written thus,

describe, disagree.

(*b*) In the following pairs of words note that the stressed vowel sound is represented by using the stroke *l* or stroke *r* instead of the hook ; thus,

ripple but repeal ; reaper but repair ; debtor but deter ; regal but regale.

(*c*) Similarly when a distinct vowel sound occurs between *l* or *r* and a preceding consonant, and no other consonant stroke occurs in the word, the stroke is used for *l* or *r* and not the hook ; thus,

peal, par, scale, scar, spell, spear.

32. Intervening Vowels Indicated. To avoid a long or awkward outline, a dot vowel between a stroke and an initial hook is indicated by writing a *small circle*, instead of the dot, *after* or *before* the stroke ; thus,

⟋ *parcel,* ⟋— *chair-maker,* ⟋ *cheerily.*

An intervening dash vowel is indicated by writing the dash at the beginning or end of the hooked form for a first or third-place vowel respectively, and through the hooked form for a second-place vowel ; thus,

⟋ *George,* ⟋ *church,* ⟋ *troubadour.*

Note also ⟋ *mixture.* It is seldom necessary to vocalize in this way.

Exercise 37
Read, copy, and transcribe

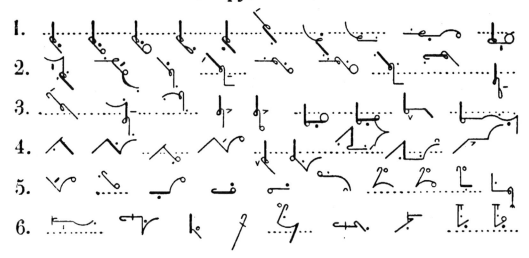

Exercise 38
Write in Shorthand

1. Advisable, disclosed, plausible, traceable, instil, musical, extol, exploded.
2. Extra, extreme, extremely, mystery, reciter, expressed, mistrust, extracted.
3. Prospers, destroyed, disgrace, disgraced, outsider, retail, details, retire.

4. Bills, gulls, pools, deals, parley, purchase, purchases, neighborhood.

5. Charming, culture, carpet, carpets, parcel, parcels, courtesy, recorded.

6. Faculty, faculties, discourse, discourage, discouraged, direct, directed, fixtures.

GRAMMALOGS

people ;   *belief-ve-d ;*   *tell,*   *till ;*   *deliver-ed-y ;*   *largely ;*   *call,*   *equal-ly ;*   *truth ;*   *doctor,*   *dear,*   *during ;*   *principal-le-ly ;*   *liberty,*   *member* or *remember-ed,*   *number-ed ;*   *larger ;*   *care ;*   *surprise,*   *surprised.*

PHRASES

by all ;   *at all ;*   *I believe.*

Exercise 39

Read, copy, and transcribe

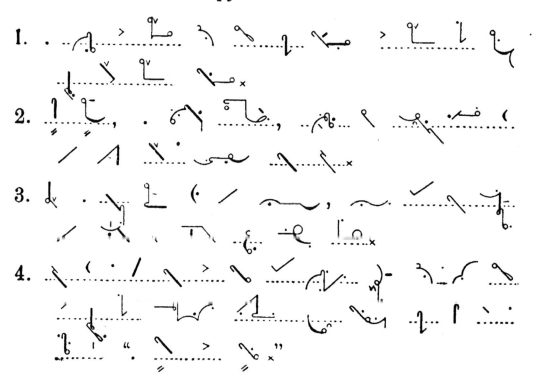

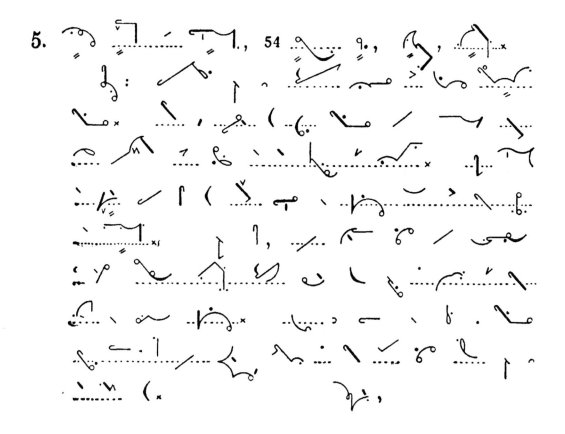

Exercise 40

Write in Shorthand

1. *It-is equally* true *that-the* recent decreases *in-the* prices *of-the* cheaper fabrics *are expected to*-result *in* increased sales.

2. Extra *care* must *be* exercised by-*all* not *to* obstruct *the* passage *of-the* bills relating *to-the* labor problems now facing us.

3. *Several members of-the* college faculty expressed *the belief that-it-was* absolutely necessary *to*-take proper steps *to*-bring about harmony *in-the* ranks *of* capital *and* labor.

4. *Our* industry prospers *because of-the* direct methods *we* employ *with* purchasers. *We tell-them* only *the truth when-we* describe *our* products, *and, as a* result, *the* list *of* satisfied buyers grows *larger and larger* each week.

5. Messrs. Peters & Blake,

Battle, Alberta.

Dear-Sirs :

Since *you have* expressed *a* desire *to* know *something of-our* silk waists *and* dresses, *we*-take-*the-liberty of* inviting *you* to-*our* offices *and* salesrooms, at 65 Worth Street, *in-your* city. *We-shall-be*-pleased *to* show samples *of-our* styles *for-this* season.   *Our* designs avoid *all* extremes *in* styles *without any* loss *of*-charm. *Al*ready record sales *are* reported by-*the* jobbers. Both wholesale *and* retail dealers *are* supplied at prices *that*-make *a* strong appeal *to-them*.

Please *acknowledge-the* receipt *of-our* catalog, *which-we-have-sent to-you* by parcel-post *to*-day. ·

Yours-truly,

SUMMARY

1. Hook *l*, added to straight strokes, is written with the left motion, and circle *s* is prefixed by writing the circle inside the hook.

2. Hook *r*, added to straight strokes, is written with the right motion, and the circles *s* and *sw* and the *st* loop are prefixed by writing the circle or loop on the *r* side of the straight stroke.

3. Strokes initially hooked for *l* or *r* are vocalized and read like single strokes.

4. A circle and hook occurring medially must both be shown.

5. A vowel may be indicated between an initial hook and a stroke consonant (*a*) by writing a small circle for a dot vowel, and (*b*) by writing a dash vowel-sign through the stroke consonant.

LESSON IX

33. Initial Hook for R to Curves. A *small* initial hook, written inside the curve, adds *r* to the curves *f, v, th, TH, sh, zh, m* and *n ;* thus,

ᐧ *fr,* ᐧ *vr,* (*th r,* (*TH r,*) *sh r,*) *zh r,* ᐧ *mr,* ᐧ *nr.*

(*a*) These double consonants are vocalized and read like single consonants. The circle *s* is prefixed to them as shown in the following illustrations—

ᐧ *off,* ᐧ *offer,* ᐧ *suffer ;* ᐧ *eve,* ᐧ *ever,* ᐧ *sever ;* ᐧ *calm,* ᐧ *calmer ;* -(*oath,* ᐧ *author ;* -(*other,* ᐧ *soother ;* ᐧ *shoe,* ᐧ *shrew ;* ᐧ *pusher,* ᐧ *fisher ;*) *measure ;* ᐧ *resume,* ᐧ *resumer ;* ᐧ *inn,* ᐧ *inner,* ᐧ *sinner ;* ᐧ *furnace,* ᐧ *sufferance.*

(*b*) The double consonant) *shr* is written *downward only.*

(*c*) The sign ᐧ is employed for the representation of either *ng-kr* or *ng-gr ;* as

ᐧ *bang,* ᐧ *banker,* ᐧ *drinker,* ᐧ *conquer.*

(*d*) Words ending in *ng-r* are represented thus,

ᐧ *singer,* ᐧ *swinger,* ᐧ *ringer.*

34. Initial Hook for L to Curves. A *large* initial hook, written inside the curve, adds *l* to the curves *f, v, th, TH, sh, m* and *n ;* thus,

ᐧ *fl,* ᐧ *vl,* (*th l,* (*TH l,* ᐧ (up) *sh l,* ᐧ *ml,* ᐧ *nl.*

(*a*) The double consonant ᐧ *sh l* is written *upward only.*

(*b*) The explanations stated in paragraphs **31** and **32** with regard to the medial use of circles and hooks, the use of the hook or stroke for *l* and *r*, and the representation of intervening vowels, are applicable to the curved strokes as well as to the straight strokes.

(*c*) The following words illustrate the use of these double consonants. The circle *s* is prefixed in the manner shown.

foe,   flow,   float,   flame;   eve,   evil, civil;   peace,   peaceful;   oath,   Ethel; pale,   palatial;   fish,   official;   Cam, camel;   O'Donnell.

Exercise 41

Read, copy, and transcribe

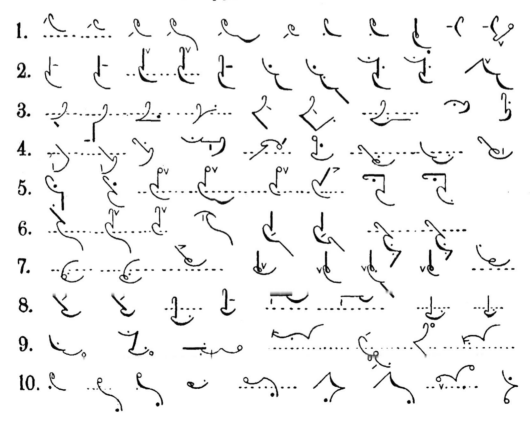

Exercise 42

Write in Shorthand

1. Flowed, flap, flabby, flank, flanker, flare, flask, fledge.
2. Ash, usher, ushering, shrank, clasher, splasher, dasher.
3. Measure, treasure, closure, enclosure, leisure, leisurely.
4. Gram, grammar, climb, climber, schemer, claim, claimer.
5. Pawner, diner, joiner, keener, cleaner, thinker, stronger.
6. Savor, summer, sooner, dishonor, dishonored, dishonorable, external.
7. Eternal, penalty, final, manner, briefly, bravely, shimmer.
8. Pressure, brusher, shelves, shellac, shrivel, bushel, racial.
9. Nurse, nourish, ignores, north, shilling, enormous, personality.
10. Personnel, canal, revile, refill, tenure, small, snare.

35. Alternative Forms. The hooked forms ⌣ *fr*, ⌣ *vr*, (*th r*, (*TH r*, *turned over to the right*, are employed as alternative signs for these double consonants ; thus,

⌣⌐ *fr*, ⌣⌐ *vr*, ( ) *th r*, ( ) *TH r*.

(*a*) When a sign for *fr*, *vr*, *th r*, *TH r*, etc., is joined to another stroke, that form is used which joins most easily. As a general rule, the left curve is joined to a stroke written *towards the left*, and the right curve when joined to a stroke written *towards the right* ; thus,

Jefferson, *average*, *proffer*, *cover*, *covered*, *weather*, *bother*, *bothered*.

(*b*) If the double consonant stands alone, the *left* curve is written *if a vowel precedes*, and the *right* curve *if a vowel does not precede* ; thus,

affray, *fray* ; *ever*, *verse* ; *author*, *throw*.

(c) The signs ⌒ *fl* and ⌒ *vl* are also *turned over to the right*, to provide alternative signs for these double consonants. The right curves ⌒ and ⌒ are used only *when following* — *k*, — *g*, ⌣ *n*, or the straight upstrokes thus,

⌒ *scuffle*, ⌒ *gravel*, ⌒ *novel*, ⌒ *rival*.

Exercise 43

Read, copy, and transcribe

1.
2.
3.
4.

Exercise 44

Write in Shorthand

1. Frock, freak, frail, forgot, refreshed, floated, rivers.
2. Braver, brothers, hemisphere, atmosphere, marvel, frolic.
3. Flee, flight, flights, freezes, floats, offered, either.
4. Reflect, inflict, inflicts, removal, upheaval, flurry, flames.

GRAMMALOGS

⌒ *over*, ⌒ *however* ; ⌒ *valuation* ;) *their* or *there* ;) *therefore* ; ⌒ *from* ; ⌒ *very* ;) *sure* ;) *pleasure* ; ⌒ *more* or *remark-ed*, ⌒ *remarkable-y*, ⌒ *Mr.* or *mere* ; ⌣ *nor*, ⌣ *near*.

PHRASES

) *they are*, ⌣ *in our*.

Exercise 45

Read, copy, and transcribe

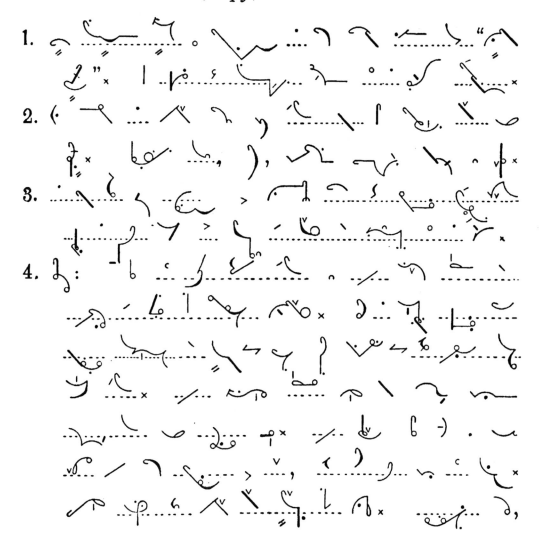

Exercise 46

Write in Shorthand

1. *In-our* haste *we*-must not *over*look certain facts regarding-*the* enormous outlay involved if-*we* accept these proposals.

2. Through *our* system *of* weekly reports *to-the* home office *we-have* gathered enough evidence *to* assure us *that-there*-will-*be* no upheaval *in-the* ranks *of-our* workers *for*-some time.

3. Intense rivalry *in-the* automobile industry *has* resulted *this year in a* marvelous increase *in* business *for* everybody. *Although* they-*are all* highly pleased *with-the* figures, many dealers feel *sure* they-will-*be* doubled *next year.*

4. *Dear Mr.* Frost :

We-have received *your* note regarding *what you* term *an* unwarranted increase *in-the* tax *valuation of-your* property located at 36 Broad Street, *in-this* city. *You*-may-*be-sure the* figures *are* correct, *for-the* tax appraisers make *a very-care*ful study *of*-each parcel before-*the* total *valuation is* arrived at. *The regular* method *of*-procedure *was* employed *in-your*-case, *and Mr.* Frank Traynor, *the* tax expert *in-our* office, *is* at *your* service *to*-go *over-the* entire problem *with you.*

Very-truly-*yours,*   (94)

Summary

1, A small initial hook adds *r* to curves ; a large initial hook adds *l*.

2. There are alternative forms for *fr, vr, th r, TH r, fl* and *vl*.

3. *Sh r* is written downward only, and *sh l* is written upward only.

LESSON X

36. Final Hook for N. A small final hook, written with the right motion, adds *n* to all straight strokes, and written inside the curves, adds *n* to curves. Whenever convenient, the *n* hook is used in the middle of a word also ; thus,

pay, *pain,* *bane,* *tone,* *done,* *chain,*

Jane, *cane,* *gain,* *feign,* *vain,* *thin,*

thine, *assign,* *zone,* *shown,* *mine,* *nine,*

line, *earn,* *Rhine,* *wine,* *yawn,* *hone,*

pining, *punish,* *banish,* *dining,* *refinery.*

Exercise 47

Write in Shorthand

1. Pan, span, plain, planning, sprain, brown, train, strain.
2. Forgotten, restrain, sudden, coin, coining, cleaning, turn, begin, region.
3. Soften, remain, remaining, machine, assign, assigning, horn, earnest.
4. Linen, stolen, refine, earthen, refrain, discern, woven, varnish.
5. Discipline, plenty, obtaining, vanish, finished, furnish, furnished, fringe.

(*a*) A circle or loop written on the *n* side of a straight stroke includes the hook *n* ; thus,

pay, *pain,* *pains,* *pun,* *puns,* *punster,*

punsters ; *ten,* *tense,* *tenses ;* *chain,* *chains,*

chances, *chanced ;* *wince,* *winced,* *winces.*

55

(*b*) The small circle is written inside the *n* hook attached to a curve, and adds the heavy sound of *z* only ; thus,

ᔕ *fine,* ᔕ *fines ;* ᔕ *van,* ᔕ *vans ;* ᔑ *assign,* ᔑ *assigns ;* ᔗ *moan,* ᔗ *moans ;* ᔘ *line,* ᔘ *lines.*

(*c*) **The light sound -*ence*, after a curved stroke.** The stroke *n*, with the circle or loop added, must be used in words like

ᔙ *fence,* ᔙ *fences,* ᔙ *fenced ;* ᔚ *mince,* ᔛ *romance,* ᔜ *allowance.*

Exercise 48

Write in Shorthand

1. Pans, plans, explains, prance, prances, pranced, entrance, entrances.
2. Bones, ribbons, drains, residences, resistance, distances, regions, chances.
3. Wagons, weakens, burns, coupons, urchins, cleanses, against, appliances.
4. Refines, remains, earns, summons, frowns, shrines, horns, women's.
5. Evinced, prominence, alliance, allowances, finance, sciences, renounced, minces.

37. **Final Hook for F, V.** A small final hook, written with the left motion, adds *f* or *v* to straight strokes. The circle *s* is added to this hook as shown, and when convenient the hook is used in the middle of a word ; thus,

ᔝ *pay,* ᔞ *pave,* ᔟ *paving,* ᔠ *paves ;* ᔡ *braves,* ᔢ *braving ;* ᔣ *tough,* ᔤ *deaf,* ᔥ *define ;* ᔦ *chafe,* ᔧ *chafes ;* ᔨ *cuff,* ᔩ *cuffs ;* ᔪ *gave,* ᔫ *rave,* ᔬ *raves ;* ᔭ *wave,* ᔮ *waves ;* ᔯ *heave,* ᔰ *heaves ;* ᔱ *driving,* ᔲ *proving.*

(*a*) A stroke which is finally hooked may be halved to add either *t* or *d*. In such outlines the hook is read *before* the *t* or *d* ; thus,

⟍ *pain,* ⟍ *paint* or *pained,* ⟍ *paints ;* ⟍ *fine,* ⟍ *find,*

⟍ *finds ;* ⟋ *wave,* ⟋ *waft ;* ⟋ *raved.*

38. Final Vowel Sound. Neither the hook *n* nor the hook *f-v* is used finally if a vowel sound follows—

⟍ *puny,* ⟍ *coffee,* ⟍ *funny,* ⟍ *wavy,* ⟍ *avenue.*

(*a*) **Intervening Vowels.** Neither of these hooks is used if a vowel occurs between *n* or *f-v* and a following sound that is represented by a circle or a loop ; thus,

⟍ *bones,* but ⟍ *bonus,* ⟍ *bonuses,* ⟍ *bannister ;*

⟋ *raves,* but ⟋ *revise,* ⟋ *revises,* ⟋ *revised ;*

⟿ *men's,* but ⟿ *menace,* ⟿ *menaces,* ⟿ *menaced,*

⟿ *minister.*

Exercise 49

Read, copy, and transcribe

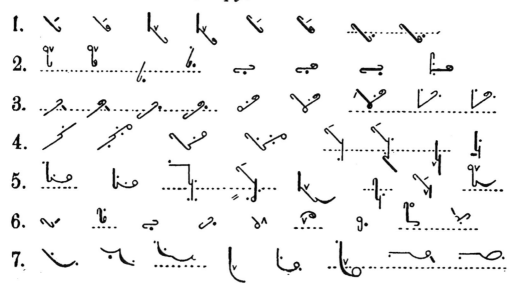

Exercise 50

Write in Shorthand

1. Puff, puffing, puffs, disprove, define, defining, definite.
2. Proof, proofs, prove, proving, reproving, deaf, devote.
3. Win, wind, winds, line, lined, lend, lends, lands.
4. Accidents, explained, returned, planned, cleaned, grants, graft, engraved, observed, reprieved.
5. Bone, bony, tune, tiny, brain, brainy, rough, review.
6. Services, refuses, devised, defaces, prefaces, professed.
7. Genus, denies, ransom, winsome, lonesome, dancer.

GRAMMALOGS AND CONTRACTIONS

❯ been, ⌡ general-ly, ⌣ within, (southern, ‿ northern, ‿ opinion, ❯ balance, ∫ deliverance, ‿ signify-ied-ficant, ‿ significance, ❯ behalf, ⌊ advantage, ⌐ difficult, ⌊ difficulty.

PHRASES

⌡ had been, ❯ have been, ⌐ out of, ∕ which have, ι who have, ⌡ at once.

Exercise 51

Read, copy, and transcribe

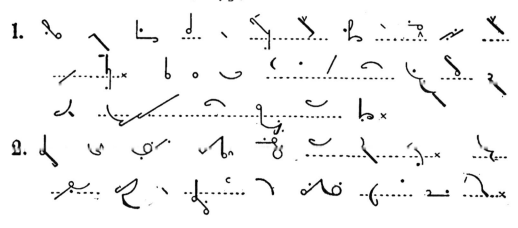

3.

4.

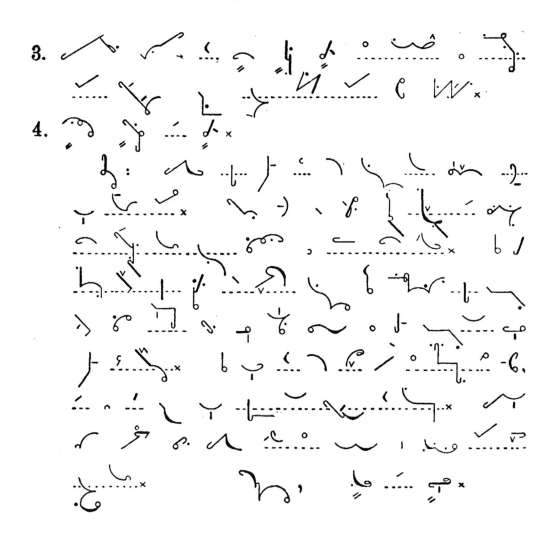

Exercise 52

Write in Shorthand

1. *We-have signified our* desire *to* appear before-*the* local authorities *to* state *our opinion* regarding-*the* proposed telephone *and* telegraph rates.

2. Oil producers *have-been* forced *to-call on-their* reserve supplies *to*-meet-*the remarkable* demand *for* gasoline by users throughout-*the* entire country.

3. *We-have-been* advised by *our insurance* agents *that-you wish to*-take *advantage of-the* liberal dividend returns offered *in-our* recent stock issue.

4. Messrs. Evans & Groves,

Dear-Sirs :

We would-be ungrateful indeed if-*we*-did not accept *your* kind hint. *As a* direct result *we-have* planned *a* series *of*-trips *for our* salesmen *which*-will bring *them into* closer touch *with our* customers *all-over* Canada. *Our* men leave Toronto at-once *with* samples *of-our* advance lines. They-will explain *to-you the* reasons *for-the* apparent slackness *we-have* shown *during-the* past season. *It-has-been* one *of-much* stress *for* us, *and we-are*-inclined-*to-think you*-will make-*the* proper allowances *when you* hear *our* story.

You-will-*be*-glad *to*-learn *that-the* new lines *to be* shown *to-you have-been* favorably received *in-the northern* states. They-*are of* splendid value, *and are* sold at prices *that give* us *a very*-low margin *of*-profit.

Yours-very-truly,

SUMMARY

1. The hook *n* added to straight strokes is written with the right motion, and the hook *f* or *v* with the left motion.

2. The hook *n* is written inside of curves.

3. A final circle or loop written with the right motion to straight strokes includes the hook *n*.

4. Circle *s* is written inside of hooks attached to curves.

5. After a curve the stroke *n* must be employed in the light sounds of *ence,* etc.

6. A stroke which is finally hooked may be halved for either *t* or *d*.

7. Hooks *n, f-v* are not used finally if the word ends with a vowel.

LESSON XI

39. Final Hook for SHUN. A large final hook adds *shun* to curves or straight strokes ; thus,

vision, visionary ; nation, national ; mission, missioner ; passion, auction, traction.

As indicated, the *shun* hook is used in the middle of a word whenever a good joining is obtained, and is always written inside of curves.

40. When attached to straight strokes it is written as follows—

(*a*) On the side opposite to an initial hook or circle; thus,

oppression, repression, repletion, Grecian, station, hesitation, section, dissection, secretion, desecration.

(*b*) Away from the curve when added to ___ or ___ following the curves ⌣, ⌣ or ⌐ (up) as

fiction, vacation, location, legation.

These two rules have a balancing effect on the outlines and tend to preserve the straightness of the strokes.

(*c*) On the side opposite to the last vowel when added to a straight stroke which has no initial attachment ; thus,

potion, option ; auction, caution ; operation, portion.

(In such words the last vowel is indicated without actually writing the vowel-sign.)

(*d*) On the right side of the simple stroke | | / as

⁁ *rotation,* ⁀ *notation,* ⌣ *addition,* ⌒ *magician.*

Since the last **vo**wel always occurs AFTER | | / in such words, there **is** no need to indicate that fact.

A stroke that is finally hooked for *shun* may be halved to add either *t* or *d*, as

⌣ *fashioned,* ⌒ *motioned*

Exercise 53

Write in Shorthand

1. Missions, missionary, infusion, invasion, solution, solutions, professional.
2. Permission, stipulation, suffusion, supervision, ammunition, elimination, orations.
3. Probation, traditions, inception, seclusion, hesitation, frustration, politicians, perfection.
4. Reduction, occasions, occasional, adoption, reparation, elections.
5. Eviction, vocations, vocational, imitation, magicians, rendition.
6. Partitioned, rationed, auctioned, occasioned, provisioned.

GRAMMALOGS AND CONTRACTIONS

＼ *public-sh-ed,* ＼ *publication;* ＼ *subject-ed,* ＼ *subjective,*

＼ *subjection;* ⌐ *signification;* ＼— *subscribe-d,*

＼⌐ *subscription;* ⌒ *inform-ed,* ⌒ *informer,*

⌐ *information;* ⋀ *represent-ed,* ⋀ *representative,*

⋀ *representation.*

Exercise 54

Read, copy, and transcribe

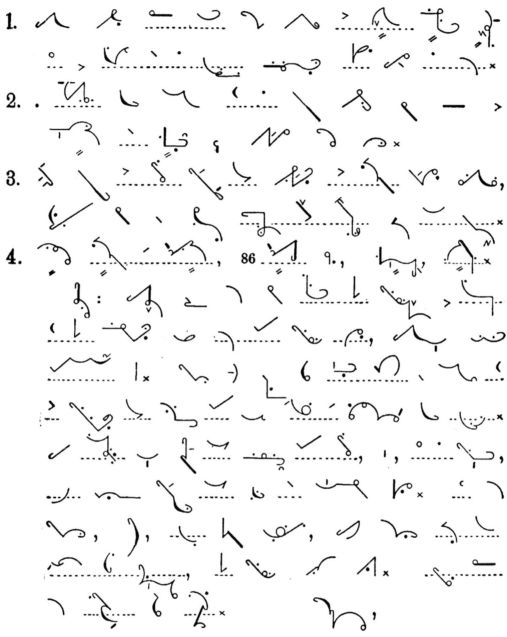

Exercise 55

Write in Shorthand

1. They-*have* *al*ready expressed *their* intention *to subscribe*
liberally *to-the* movement *which* seeks *to* enforce *the*
adoption *of* safety devices *for-the* prevention *of*
collisions.

2. Unfortunately *we-can* attach little or no *signification to-the* author's *representations of-his-own* book. *Our subscription and* sales departments both report *a very* weak market *for-it as* yet.

3. *Our informer, in-this*-instance, *is Mr.* Frank Wiggins, *the special* news *representative in* foreign capitals. *His* impressions *of-the* last sessions *of-the* peace parley *have* won-*the* warm approbation *of-the* leading statesmen *in* foreign countries.

4. Messrs. Jones *&* Smith,

      54 Spruce Avenue, Brandon, Manitoba.

    Dear-Sirs :

    Your representative visited us *yesterday, and* gave us full *information* regarding *your publications. We*-were-not, *however,* ready at-*the* moment *to subscribe for any of*-these, *though-we* hope *to*-take *several of-the* new editions *of-your* older texts *in a* week or-*two.* Please express *to* us at-once four copies each *of "* The Dictionary *of* Education," " *Public* Finance," " Labor *Representation on Public* Bodies," *and* " Rational Psychology."

    Kindly *inform our* Fiction Department *as to-the* best terms upon-*which you-can* supply gross lots *of-your* new novels " Woman *in Subjection,"* by Armstrong, *and* " The Informer," by Brown. *Yours very*-truly, (118)

41. SHUN following Circles S or NS and a Vowel. In words like *position* and *transition*, where the sound of *shun* follows the circle *s* and a vowel, *shun* is expressed by a small hook following the sweep of the circle ; thus,

    pose,   *position ;*   *sense,*   *sensation ;*

    dispense,   *dispensation ;*   *transitional.*

(Note that this hook is also used medially.)

First-place vowels do not occur between circle *s* and *shun*. Second-place vowels are read between circle *s* and *shun* when the hook is left unvocalized, as ⟋ *procession*, ⟋ *processional* ; and third-place vowels are indicated by writing the vowel sign outside the hook. A final *s* circle may be written inside this hook ; thus,

⟋ *decision*, ⟋ *supposition*, ⟋ *suppositions*.

42. Words ending in -uation or -uition. The stroke *sh* and hook *n* are generally employed for these terminations, as in the words ⟋ *extenuation*, ⟋ *intuition*. It is permissible to use the large hook in ⟋ *perpetuation*, ⟋ *fluctuation*, and similar words, in order to avoid a too lengthy outline. There are comparatively few words of this class.

Exercise 56
Read, copy, and transcribe

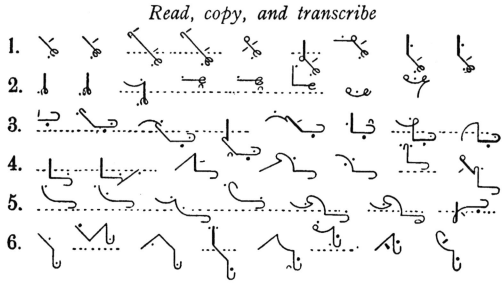

Exercise 57
Write in Shorthand

1. Possession, procession, processional, physician, physicians.
2. Succession, taxation, vexation, secession, musicians.
3. Lotion, repulsion, expulsion, stipulation, stipulations.

5—(445) *Cass.*

4. Ration, aberration, saturation, derision, negation.
5. Attrition, intrusion, intrusions, penetration, cushions.
6. Notation, mutation, exultation, laudation, logician.

GRAMMALOGS AND CONTRACTIONS

satisfaction, satisfactory; organization, organize-d; generalization, justification; responsible-ility, irresponsible-ility; circumstance, circumstances, circumstantial.

Exercise 58

Read, copy, and transcribe

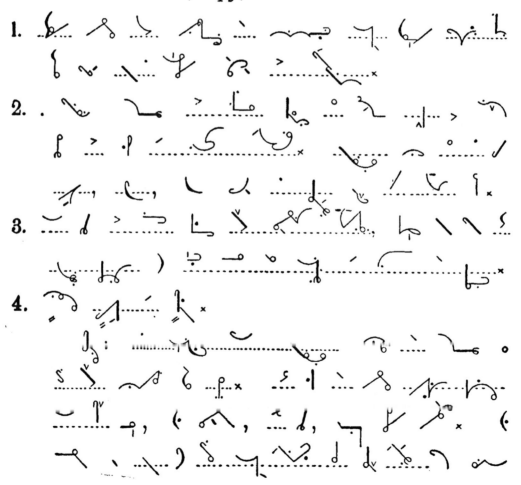

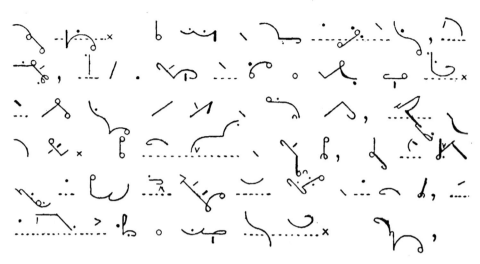

Exercise 59

Write in Shorthand

1. Despite *the* accusations against *him and-the* strong chain *of circumstantial* evidence *which-was* forged by-*the* attorneys *for-the* prosecution, *the* prisoner's counsel felt little worry about proving *his* client's innocence.

2. *Circumstances* force us *to organize a* nation-wide movement *whose* purpose *it*-will-*be* to secure freedom *for all* political prisoners.

3. *The* final decision against *his* promotion *was*-due *to-his irresponsibility,* many-instances *of-which had-been* brought *to-their* attention *on several different* occasions.

4. *Dear*-Sir :

We-regret *to inform-you that your* application *for* admission *to-the* College *of* Physicians *and* Surgeons *has-been* denied. *It-is a* rule *of-our organization,* strictly enforced, *that when-the* slightest suspicion *is* cast upon *an* applicant, he-may not *be* permitted *to* pursue *any* studies at-*this* institution.   *Your* references were *very-carefully* looked *into, and, much to-our surprise, we*-received certain *information that* reflects upon *your* integrity *in* no uncertain manner. *We-are*-not at *liberty to* disclose *this information nor its* source.

Very-truly-yours,   (93)

SUMMARY

1. A large final hook written inside of curves represents *shun*.

2. The *shun* hook attached to straight strokes is written *away* from an initial attachment, or from the last vowel if there is no initial attachment.

3. The *shun* hook is written on the right side of | | /

4. When following a circle *shun* is expressed by a small hook.

5. A third-place vowel between circle *s* and *shun* is indicated by writing the vowel-sign outside the hook. When left unvocalized a second-place vowel is to be read between the *s* and *shun*.

6. The large hook is sometimes used to represent *-uation* or *-uition*.

LESSON XII

43. Compound Consonants. A large initial hook adds *w* to *k* and *g*; thus,

⌐ *calm*, ⌐ *qualm*; ⌐ *quire*, ⌐ *Maguire*;

⌐ *request*, ⌐ *sequence*, ⌐ *linguist*.

These strokes are named *Kw* and *Gw* respectively.

(*a*) A small initial hook prefixes *w* to upward *l*; thus,

⌐ *ell*, ⌐ *well*, ⌐ *unwell*, ⌐ *Stonewall*,

⌐ *woolens*, ⌐ *wealth*, ⌐ *wilts*.

This stroke is named *Wl*. The *w* hook is *always* read first.

(*b*) A large initial hook adds the aspirate *h* to *w* and *wl*; thus,

⌐ *weep*, ⌐ *whip*; ⌐ *wail*, ⌐ *whale*;

⌐ *whispered*, ⌐ *wheels*, ⌐ *meanwhile*.

These strokes are named *Whay* and *Whl* respectively.

(*c*) Downward *l* or *r* is thickened for the addition of *r* preceded by any short vowel; *m* is thickened for the addition of *p* or *b*; thus,

⌐ *full*, ⌐ *fuller*; ⌐ *scale*, ⌐ *scaler*;

⌐ *share*, ⌐ *sharer*; ⌐ *Cam*, ⌐ *camp*;

⌐ *bamboo*, ⌐ *dampen*; ⌐ *hamper*, ⌐ *slumber*.

These strokes are named *Ler*, *Rer* and *Emp* or *Emb* respectively.

(*d*) *Ler* and *Rer* are used only where a downward *l* or *r* may be used when following another consonant sound. These consonants are not used, however, if a distinct vowel intervenes, or if a vowel follows the final *r ;* as,

failure,   *foolery,*   *dealer,*   *toiler.*

(*e*) In words like *em-press, em-ploy, em-brace, em-blem,* where *pr, pl, br* or *bl* immediately follows *m* without an intervening vowel, write the *pr, pl, br* or *bl,* and not the thickened *m ;* thus,

empress,   *employ,*   *embrace,*   *emblem,*

but   *impure,*   *impel,*   *embarrass,*   *embellish.*

Exercise 60

Read, copy, and transcribe

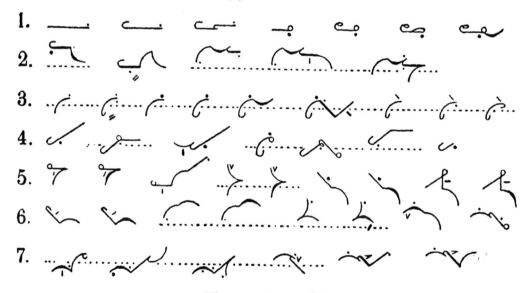

Exercise 61

Write in Shorthand

1. Cake, quake, quaker, queen, squire, square, squarer.
2. Squeal, squealer, quest, inquest, request, linguist.
3. Eel, weal, wealthy, well-known, welfare, unwell, wailed.
4. Wail, whale, whaling, whale-bone, weasel, whistle.

5. Nail, nailer, councillor, councillors, store, storer, storers.

6. Damp, hemp, trombone, clam, clamber, embody, embezzle.

7. Embargo, imposition, ambition, while, awhile, whine, whiff.

GRAMMALOGS AND CONTRACTIONS

important-ce, *improve-d-ment,* *impossible,* *improves-ments,* *whether,* *practice-d,* *practicable,* *especial-ly,* *commercial-ly,* *financial-ly,* *questionable-ly.*

Exercise 62

Read, copy, and transcribe

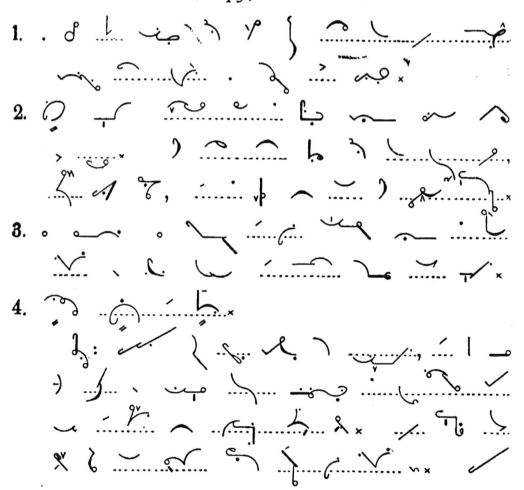

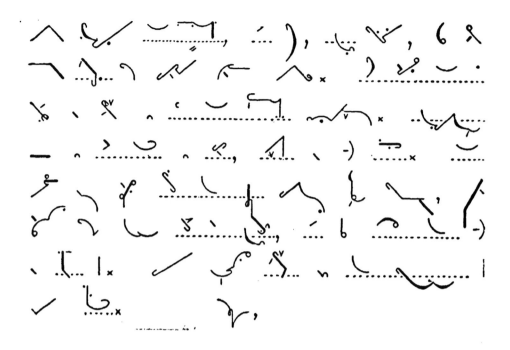

Exercise 63

Write in Shorthand

1. Many *improvements* designed *to* add *to-the* welfare *of-the* tenants *are to be* found *in-the* newer apartments now *being* built here.

2. Fully equipped *with all-the* necessary data, they began *an* intensive campaign against *the* imposition *of* high tariff rates *on* imported woolens. *Their* arguments were *very* embarrassing *to-the* opposition.

3. *Our* deliberations *on-the* ship subsidy bill *have-been* embodied *in-the* form *of a* set *of* resolutions. Copies *have-been* forwarded *to-our* representatives, *and* also *to-the* press *for publication*.

4. *Dear Mr.* Fowler :

   In accordance *with your* inquiry, *we have* looked *into-the financial* standing *of Mr.* Thomas Wheeler, *and-his general* reputation *in commercial* circles. *We*-regret *to inform-you that* many *important* facts *have come to*-light *which* stamp *him as a* man *of questionable practices in-his* business dealings.

While he acts strictly *within his* legal rights, he does-not hesitate *to*-employ methods *that would-never be* resorted *to* by men *of* un*questionable* integrity. He-*has* few intimate acquaintances or close friends, *and*-they evince little or no willingness *to*-impart *any information* about *him which*-may-*be in their* possession. *We* doubt *whether it-would-be* advisable *for-you* to entrust *to-his care the* affair *you*-mention.

Very-truly-*yours,* (126)

44. Omission of Consonants. To obtain briefer, or more facile outlines, certain medial consonants are omitted, **as** follows—

(*a*) *p* between *m* and *t* or *sh ;* thus,

presumptive, *exemption,* *resumption.*

(*b*) *k* or *g* between *ng* and *t* or *sh ;* thus,

anxious, *sanction,* *extinct.*

(*c*) *t* between circle *s* and another consonant ; thus,

postpone, *testimony,* *postage.*

Exercise 64

Write in Shorthand

1. Prompt, stamped, encamped, attempted, tempt, temptation.
2. Presumption, redemption, assumption, gumption.
3. Punctual, punctuation, puncture, junction, adjunct, extinction.
4. Perfunctory, precinct, succinct, distinction, function.
5. Postmaster, postponed, tasteful, tasteless, trustworthy, adjustment.
6. Honestly, restless, wasteful, trustful, listless, manifestly, optimistic.

CONTRACTIONS

⌒ *uniform-ly-ity,*   ⌢ *unanimous-ly,*   ‾ *executive,*

⌐ *defective,*   ⋀ *republic,*   ⋀ *republican.*

Exercise 65

Read, copy, and transcribe

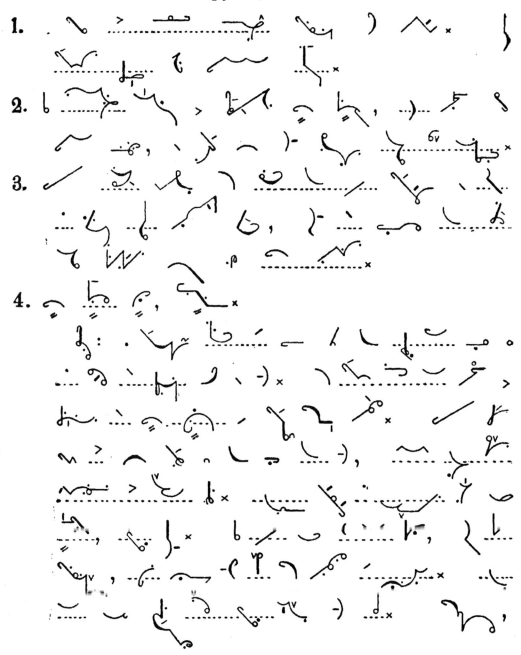

Exercise 66

Write in Shorthand

1. *A defective* wire *was responsible for-the* accident *which* resulted *in* so wasteful *a* loss *of*-property.

2. They honestly *believe it-is a* wasteful expense *to* incur, despite *the opinions* expressed *by-the* other *executives.*

3. *It-would* add *to-your* chances if-*you*-were *to*-reserve space *in* " *Commercial Organization* " *next* month.

4. *We-are* hampered *by-the* delay *in-the delivery of-the* sheets *of-the* " Life *of* Wellington " *which-we* require *for-the* new binding.

5. *The Republican* Party *is* aware *of-the* necessity *for-the* redemption *of-their* promises *for* tariff revision so freely offered before election.

6. *Mr.* John S. Hamilton :

    Dawson, Yukon.

    Dear-Sir :

    We-regret *to-have to inform-you that-there-is*-no *justification for-the* viewpoint *you have*-seen fit *to* adopt. *You* acted entirely *on-your* own *responsibility in-the* assumption *that-we would* sanction *the* prices *you* quoted *without our* authorization. *It-is impossible for* us *to* accept *the* loss involved. *Was-it* not distinctly impressed upon *you that-we* maintain *a uniform* scale *of*-prices *for all of-our* customers *in* every part *of-the* country ? *We-have* firmly *established ourselves on-that principle, and-we* expect *to*-maintain *our* reputation *as* long *as we* remain *in* business. If *any* wrong impressions *have-been* left *as a* result *of-your* action, they-must *be* stamped out at-once.

    Very-truly-*yours,* (131)

Summary

1. *W* may be added to *k, g*, and prefixed to upward *l* by an initial hook.

2. The enlargement of the initial hook of *w* and *wl* indicates the aspirate.

3. *R* is added to downward *l* and *r* by thickening these letters.

4. *P* or *b* is added to *m* by thickening that letter.

5. *P, k,* and *g* may be omitted when only slightly sounded, and *t* may be omitted when it occurs between circle *s* and another consonant.

LESSON XIII

45. The Halving Principle. The following rules have already been learned. Light strokes are halved to add *t* ; heavy strokes are halved to add *d* ; and any stroke may be halved to add either *t* or *d* when it occurs in a word of more than one syllable, when it is finally hooked, or when it has a joined final diphthong ; thus,

⌒ *rap,* ⌒ *rapt ;* ⌒ *rob,* ⌒ *robbed ;*

⎸ *vote,* ⎸ *voted ;* ⌒ *rapid,* ⌒ *rabbit,* ⌒ *rabbits ;*

⟍ *pain,* ⟍ *paint* or *pained,* ⟍ *paints ;* ⟋ *rave,* ⟋ *raved,*

⟋ *rift,* ⟋ *rifts ;* ⎸ *doubt,* ⎸ *feud.*

(*a*) Strokes of unequal length must not be joined unless a sharp angle or an attachment intervenes. Full outlines therefore must be written in words like—

⎍ *cooked,* ⟋ *judged,* ⌒ *minute,* ⎸ *effect,*

⟋ *roared,* ⌒ *locate,* ⌒ *mopped.*

Occasionally the half-length is used, but it is disjoined to make it legible, as in—

⟍ *aptness,* ⟍ *promptness.*

(*b*) Half-length *t* or *d* immediately following stroke *t* or *d* is always disjoined ; thus,

⎸ *tree,* ⎸ *treat,* ⎸ *treated ;* ⎸ *dray,* ⎸ *dread,* ⎸ *dreaded ;*

⎸ *dated,* ⎸ *tided,* ⌒ *illustrated.*

77

(c) There are only two positions for outlines consisting wholly of half-length forms, namely, *above* the line and *on* the line ; thus,

fight, fate, feet ;　light, late, lit.

Exercise 67

Read, copy, and transcribe

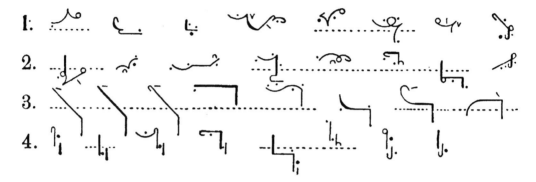

Exercise 68

Write in Shorthand

1. Spectacle, scrutinized, voluntary, multiplied, warned, weakened, elegant, sweetened.
2. Legitimate, honored, inclined, destroyed, sheltered, subsisted, behaved.
3. Vacate, terminate, minute, locked, reared, adhered, mobbed, lashed.
4. Doubted, strutted, agitated, discredited, amputated, mistreated, liquidated.

GRAMMALOGS

accord-ing or *according to,* cared ; guard, great ;

called, equalled or *cold* ; gold ; cannot ;

gentleman, gentlemen ; particular, opportunity.

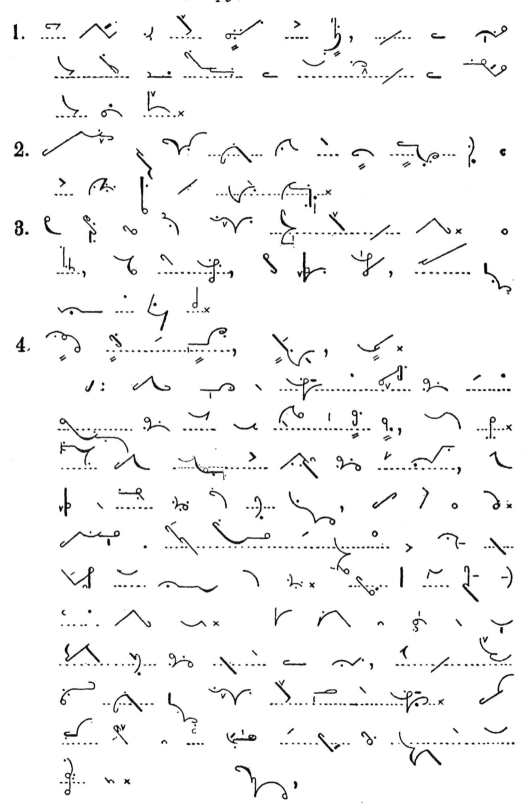

Exercise 69

Read, copy, and transcribe

1.

2.

3.

4.

Exercise 70

Write in Shorthand

1. *According-to-the* rulés *of-our* institution *we-are*-not at *liberty to* disclose *whether his* donation *was* voluntary or not.

2. *Our* business *has* multiplied enormously *during-the* past *year, and-we*-now find *it* necessary *to-guard* against *too* rapid *an* expansion.

3. *Mr.* Quinn *is-the gentleman who* suggested *that with our* present inadequate *financial* resources, *the* result *of-our* campaign *is* bound *to be* disastrous.

4. Messrs. Foote *&* Smart,
     Three Rivers, Quebec.

Gentlemen :

   Kindly accept *our thanks for-your* check *in* payment *of-our* recent shipment *to-you*. If-*we could* possibly *have* avoided *it, we would*-not-*have called*-upon *you for*-such prompt payment. *A* copy *of-our* newest illustrated catalog *has-been sent to-you to*-day. *There-is*-not-*the* slightest doubt *in-our* minds *that-it*-will please *you*. *The* preparation *of-this* booklet *has-been a great* expense *to* us, *but-we* anticipate excellent results *from it*. *You*-will-find *that* some *of-our* prices *have-been* altered, *in particular those for-the* lace embroideries. These price changes were necessitated *by-the* uncertain labor market *that* exists *in-our* industry.   *Yours-very*-truly,   (122)

46. The Consonants M, N, L, R, and the Halving Principle.
These four light strokes are not only halved for *t*, but are also halved and thickened to add *d ;* thus,

⌢ *mate,* ⌢ *made ;* ⌣ *neat,* ⌣ *need ;*

⌐ *tilt,* ⌐ *tilled ;* ⌐ *heart,* ⌐ *hard.*

(*a*) The signs ⌐ *ld* and ⌐ *rd* are always written downward, and are used without any regard to the rules for writing downward *l* or *r*. When a vowel occurs between *l-d* or *r-d*, the halving principle is not applied. Distinguishing outlines are thus obtained for pairs of similarly constructed words ; as—

⌐ *foiled*, ⌐ *followed* ; ⌐ *marred*, ⌐ *married*.

(*b*) When the sign ⌐ cannot be joined easily to a stroke, the sound of *rd* is represented by the half-sized upward *r*, as in ⌐ *lured*, ⌐ *subordinate*.

(*c*) The signs ⌐ ⌐ ⌐ and ⌐ must not be used if a vowel follows final *d* ; thus,

⌐ *mould* but ⌐ *mouldy* ; ⌐ *tarred*, but ⌐ *tardy* ;

⌐ *mud* but ⌐ *muddy* ; ⌐ *need* but ⌐ *needy*.

(*d*) The half-lengths ⌐ *rt* and ⌐ *rts* must not stand alone, as they might be mistaken for ⌐ *should* or ⌐ *and is*. Words like ⌐ *write* and ⌐ *writes* are, therefore, written with the stroke *t* as here shown.

47. The Consonant MP and NG and the Halving Principle. The strokes ⌐ and ⌐ are halved only when they are hooked, either initially or finally ; thus,

⌐ *hamper*, ⌐ *hampered*, ⌐ *scampered* ; ⌐ *impugn*, ⌐ *impugned* ; ⌐ *canker*, ⌐ *cankered*.

48. The Halving Principle in Phrasing. The halving principle is employed in phrasing to represent the words *it, not, word, would* ; thus,

⌐ *if it*, ⌐ *if it is*, ⌐ *in which it is* ; ⌐ *I am not*, ⌐ *you are not*, ⌐ *you will not*, ⌐ *you were not* ; ⌐ *in these words*, ⌐ *this would be*.

6—(445) *Can.*

Exercise 71

Read, copy, and transcribe

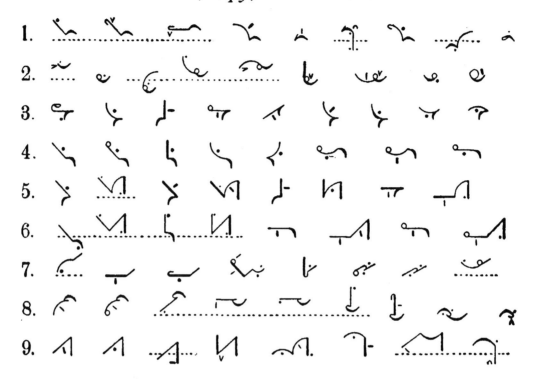

Exercise 72

Write in Shorthand

1. Seemed, summed, resumed, unharmed, modify, streamed.
2. Reasoned, fastened, thousand, resigned, kindle, syndicate.
3. Failed, scaled, kneeled, rolled, held, world, ordinary, yield.
4. Tired, dared, assured, afford, hard, steered, standard.
5. Veiled, valid, unveiled, invalid, bowled, bullied.
6. Bored, buried, bard, borrowed, stored, storied.
7. Slurred, answered, referred, preferred, ventured, wintered,
8. Campaigned, lingered, tinkered, limbered, whimpered, impend.
9. Write, writes, route, routes, stampede, imbued, longed.

GRAMMALOGS AND CONTRACTIONS

build-ing; told; tried, trade or toward,

towards; third; short; spirit; hand,

under; yard, word; school, schooled;

immediate; expenditure.

PHRASES

able to; had not or do not, did not.

Exercise 73

Read, copy, and transcribe

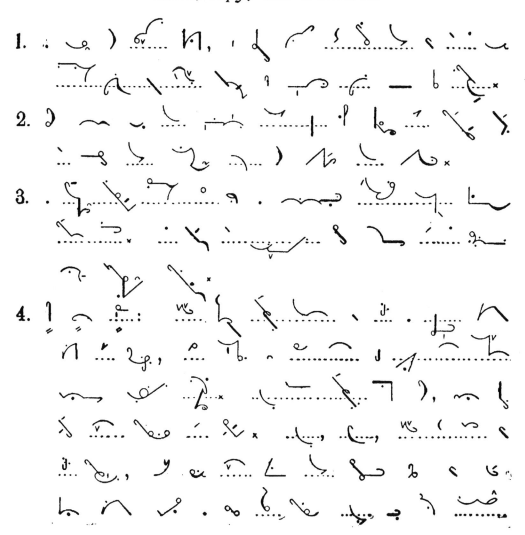

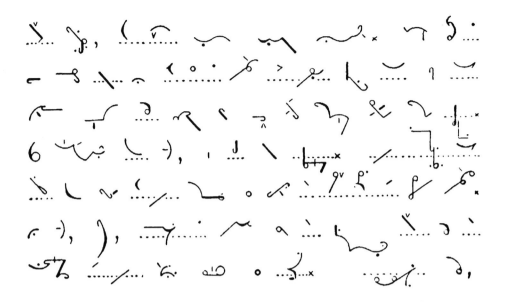

Exercise 74

Write in Shorthand

1. *We-are told that* a syndicate *has-been* formed, *and-have-been* warned also *that, in a short* space *of-*time, exports *to all* parts *of-the* world *in-our trade* will-*have to* pass through *its hands.*

2. Bankers *have* ventured *the opinion that, under-the* present arrangement *of* deferred payments *on-the* huge loan made by-*the* United-States *to* foreign countries, business, *in general*, will show a revived *spirit.*

3. *This is-the third-*time *we-have* listened *to-the* sound arguments presented by *our* subordinates *who-have tried very* hard *to-*impress upon-us *the* absolute need *of insurance* protection *for-the* ordinary laborer *as* well *as for-the* skilled workers *in-our* factory.

4. Messrs. Trent & Holland.

    Gentlemen :

    Please-*inform* us *immediately when-we-*may *expect-the* lighting fixtures *we* ordered *from-you on* October 7 last *for-the* new apartment houses *we-are-*now *building. According-to our under*standing at *that-*time *you*-were *to-deliver them towards-the* end *of-that* month, *but-you* failed *to-do* so. *It-is* distinctly *under*stood, *of*-course, *that-the* delay *was*-not intentional *on-your* part, *but-we-have* received no *word from-you* and do-not-know *your* present plans. *We-cannot* afford-*the* heavy losses involved, *and* each day's delay adds enormously *to-our* expenses. *Do*-not hesitate *to inform* us if-*you-are*-not able-*to*-make *immediate delivery*, or by-*the* end *of-this* week, at-*the very* latest. *We*-feel assured *that-you*-will-not mis*under*stand *our* attitude *under-the circumstances that* now prevail.

Very-truly-*yours*, (147)

SUMMARY

1. Light strokes are halved for the addition of *t* and heavy strokes for the addition of *d*.

2. A stroke may be halved for either *t* or *d*, (*a*) if it has a final hook or a finally joined diphthong ; (*b*) if it occurs in a word of more than one syllable.

3. Half-length *t* or *d* must be disjoined when immediately following a stroke *t* or *d*.

4. The curves ⌒ ⌣ ⌐ ⌐ may be halved and thickened for the addition of *d ;* but the half-lengths ⌐ ⌐ may not be used if a vowel separates *l-d* or *r-d*.

5. The half-lengths ⟋ *rt,* ⌐ *rts* must not stand alone. Neither is it permissible to halve ⌒ and ⌣ unless they are hooked.

6. The words *it, not, word* and *would* may be indicated by the halving principle in phrasing.

LESSON XIV

49. The Doubling Principle. Consonants are doubled **in** length to indicate the addition of *tr*, *dr*, or *TH r* ; thus,

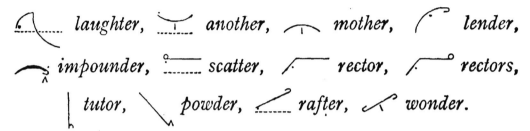

laughter, another, mother, lender, impounder, scatter, rector, rectors, tutor, powder, rafter, wonder.

(a) A final *s* circle is read *after* the termination *tr*, *dr*, or *TH r*, and a final *n* or *f-v* hook is read *before* the termination *tr*, *dr*, or *TH r* ; thus,

voters, render, renders, rafters.

(b) Double-length downstrokes are written in one position only, through the line. Double-length horizontal and upstrokes are written in the usual manner.

Exercise 75

Write in Shorthand

1. Fetter, elevator, swifter, voters, Easter, sister, shatters, smoother.
2. Motors, mother, centre, central, centralization, lighter, halter, builder.
3. Order, disorder, importer, charter, swelter, hoarder, warder, insulator.
4. Fender, vendor, thunder, inventors, remainder, cylinder, calendars.
5. Stockholder, freighter, diameter, leaseholder, householder, narrator, martyr.

50. The doubling principle must be applied to a straight stroke only when it follows a circle or stroke consonant, or has an attached diphthong or a final hook. Therefore, in words like ⌐⌐ *potter,* ⌐⌐ *reader,* ⌐⌐ *weather,* the syllable *tr, dr,* or *TH r* must be written with the hooked forms, and not indicated by the doubling principle.

Exercise 76

Write in Shorthand

1. Sceptre, sputter, sputters, sector, sectors, skater, skaters.
2. Ponder, spender, spenders, tender, tenders, plunder, plunders.
3. Binder, candor, render, surrender, wonder, rafter, wafter, hinder.
4. Drifter, grafter, squander, powder, doubter, prouder, pewter.
5. Chapter, imitator, protector, educators, duplicator, captors, indicator.

51. The character *mp* is doubled in length for the addition of *-er* ; thus,

⌐⌐ *temper,* ⌐⌐ *chamber.*

The double-length ⌐⌐ is used in all cases *except* where *mpr-mbr* immediately follows an upstroke or the horizontal ⌐⌐ *k* ; thus,

⌐⌐ *amber,* ⌐⌐ *sombre,* ⌐⌐ *vamper,* ⌐⌐ *thumper* ; but ⌐⌐ *slumber,* ⌐⌐ *hamper,* ⌐⌐ *cumber,* ⌐⌐ *scamper.*

(*a*) The character *ng* is doubled in length for the addition of *-kr* or *-gr* ; thus,

⌐⌐ *inker,* ⌐⌐ *longer.*

The double-length ‿ is used initially, and when following a circle or an upstroke ; thus,

⁀ *anchorage,* ⌣ *sinker,* ⌣ *hunger.*

In all other cases the hooked form ‿ is written ; thus,

‿ *banker,* ‿ *thinker,* ‿ *finger,* ⌐ *conquer.*

(b) The doubling principle is employed for the addition of *-ture* in a few common words like

‿ *picture,* ‿ *feature,* ‿ *signature.*

(c) When standing alone, the double-length *l* adds only the light sound *tr,* as in the words ‿ *alter,* ⌐ *letters.* Words like ‿ *louder* and ⌐ *leather* are written as here shown. In words like ⌐ *entry,* ‿ *powdery,* ‿ *feathery,* where a vowel follows final *tr, dr,* or *TH r,* the doubling principle is not employed.

52. Past Tenses. The halving principle is employed in past tenses ; thus,

⌐ *matter,* ⌐ *mattered ;* ‿ *ponder,* ‿ *pondered ;* ⟋ *render,* ⟋ *rendered ;* ‿ *temper,* ‿ *tempered ;* ‿ *linger,* ‿ *lingered.*

53. The Doubling Principle in Phrasing. This principle is used in phrases to add the words *there, their, other* and *dear ;* thus,

⟋ *I am sure there is,* ‿ *in their own way,* ‿ *take their way,* ‿ *for some other,* ⌐ *my dear sir.*

Exercise 77

Read, copy, and transcribe

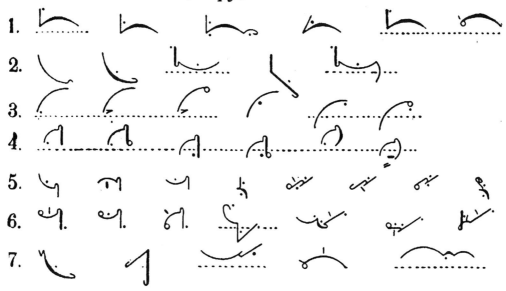

Exercise 78

Write in Shorthand

1. Bumper, jumper, timber, amber, Cumberland.
2. Scamper, scampered, hanker, hankered, drinker.
3. Nature, natural, naturalization, armature, armatures.
4. Lighter, lighters, louder, slaughter, slighter.
5. Ordered, muttered, squandered, encountered, altered.
6. Quandary, boundary, wintry, lottery, poultry, votary.
7. We-shall-be-there ; you-will-be-there ; has-been-there ; to-make-their ; in-their-opinion ; of-some-other.

GRAMMALOGS AND CONTRACTIONS

rather or *writer,* *wonderful-ly,* *influential-ly ;*
character, *characteristic ;* *interest ;*
respect-ed, *respectful,* *prejudice-d-ial ;*
advertise-d-ment *telegram ;* *telegraphic ;*
arbitrate, *arbitrary,* *arbitration ;*
discharge-d ; *certificate.*

Exercise 79

Read, copy, and transcribe

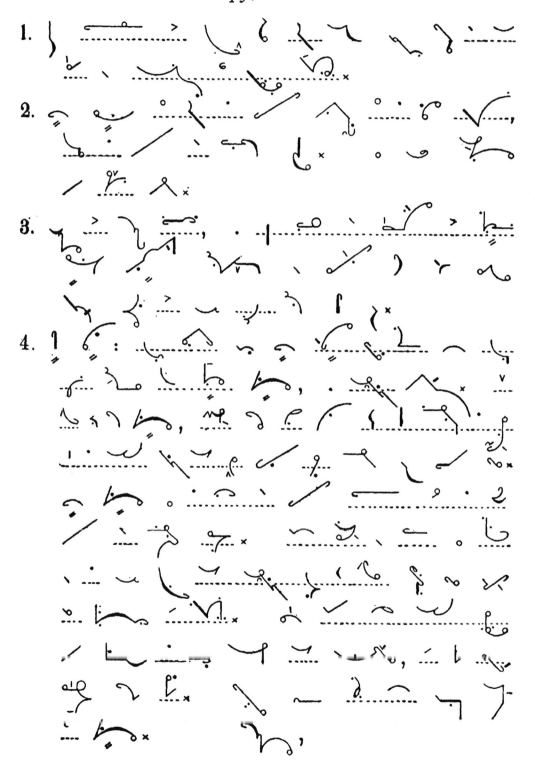

Exercise 80

Write in Shorthand

1. New rates, sanctioned by-*the* Inter-Provincial Commerce Commission, *for* telephone messages, *telegrams and telegraphic* letters, were announced by-*the* Bell Telephone Company, *to*-take effect *immediately.*

2. *Although-the* reporter's attitude *was very respectful, Mr.* Felter, *the* prosecutor *in-the* famous murder trial, displayed evidences *of* ill-temper throughout-*the* interview.

3. After-*he had discharged all-his* obligations *to-the* numerous creditors *of-the* firm, *Mr.* Anderson, *in a special* letter, announced *that a* new *organization would-be* effected *immediately.*

4. *Dear Mr.* Chamberlain :

Every car *owner should-be interested in-the* latest models *of-the* Porter six cylinder motor-car. *Our* engineers *and* designers *have* turned out *a* product *that-is-the* sensation *of-the* motor world. Shareholders *as* well *as* directors *of-the* corporation *have* expressed *the opinion that*-these *wonderful* models will revolutionize *the* automobile industry. *On all-our* models, *the* fenders *and* motor bonnet *have-been* enameled by *a* new process *that* guarantees long wear, *and gives-the* car *a* beautiful finish *and* appearance. *The* engine responds *to-the* slightest touch *of-the* accelerator. Orders *have-been* received far *beyond our* present capacity, *and-the* future *of-the* " Porter Six " *is* fully assured. *Come in and* see *it for your*self.

Very-truly-*yours,*   (126)

SUMMARY

1. The sound of *tr*, *dr*, or *TH r* is indicated by doubling a straight stroke which has an initial circle, a final hook or diphthong, or which follows another stroke.

2. Generally, curves may be doubled for the addition of *tr*, *dr*, or *TH r* ; but (*a*) the curve ⌒ *mp* is doubled for the addition of -*er* only ; and (*b*) the curve ⌣ *ng* is doubled for the addition of -*kr* or -*gr*.

3. The syllable -*ture* is indicated by doubling in a few common words.

4. Double-length *l*, standing alone, adds the light sound *tr* only.

5. The doubling principle is not employed when a vowel follows final *tr*, *dr*, or *TH r*.

6. In phrasing the words *there, their, other,* and *dear* are indicated by the doubling principle.

LESSON XV

54. Prefixes. The prefix or syllable *con-*, *com-*, or *cum-*, is indicated by a light dot written first at the *beginning* of an outline, or by writing two consonants close to each other; thus,

⌣ *commence*, ⌣ *recommence*, ⌐ *connected*,

⌐ *disconnected*, ⌐ *comply*, ⌐ *you will comply*,

ɟ *content*, ⌐ *I am content*, ⌐ *recognize*, ⌐ *recognition*.

The last two illustrations show how *cog-* is represented in the middle of a word.

(*a*) In words beginning with the dot *com-* or *con-* the position of the outline is governed by the first vowel after the prefix; thus,

⌐ *conspire*, ⌐ *confuse*.

(*b*) *Accom-* is expressed by a joined or disjoined *k*; thus,

⌐ *accommodation*, ⌐ *accommodate*, ⌐ *accomplish*.

(*c*) *Intro-* is expressed by double-length ⌣ *n*, the sign being joined where convenient; thus,

⌐ *introduce*, ⌐ *introduces*.

(*d*) *Magna-*, *magni-*, or *magne-* is expressed by a disjoined *m*; thus,

⌐ *magnanimous*, ⌐ *magnify*, ⌐ *magnetize*.

Exercise 81
Read, copy, and transcribe

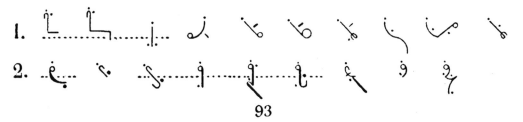

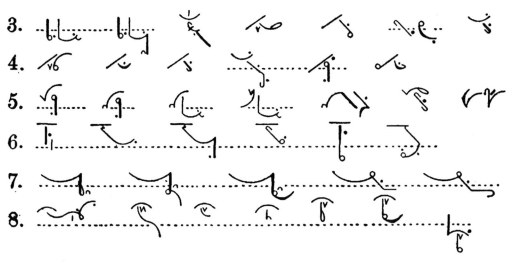

Exercise 82

Write in Shorthand

1. Control, controlling, comprise, comprised, compound, complicate, compassion, compel, compelled.
2. Complain, complained, consisted, consists, compensate, consoled, compulsory, concur.
3. Disconnect, disconnected, incomplete, circumnavigation, circumspect, recognition.
4. Inconstant, uncontrolled, incompleted, *over*-confident, recommendation, misconception.
5. *And-the*-contents, if-*the*-committee, *their*-conduct, I-must-consider, *we-have-their*-complaint.
6. Accomplished, accomplishment, accomplisher, accompanies, accomplices.
7. Introspected, introspective, introvert, introductive, introductory.
8. Magnificent, magnificence, magnificently, magnetizer, magnifying, demagnetized.

(*e*) *Self-* is indicated by a disjoined small circle, and *self-con-* is indicated by writing the circle *s* in the place of the " con " dot ; thus,

    ↄ self-defence,   self-love,   self-control,   self-conscious.

(*f*) *In-*, when preceding the circled letters ⌐ ᷍ ᷍ , is expressed by a small hook written in the direction of the circle which it precedes ; thus,

⌐ *instructed,* ⌐ *inscriber,* ⌐ *inhabit.*

(*g*) *Trans-* may be contracted in many words by omitting the *n ;* thus,

⌐ *transfer,* ⌐ *translator,* ⌐ *transmission.*

55. Negative Words. When the prefix *in-* signifies *not,* it is always expressed by the stroke *n,* as in ⌐ *inhuman.* Other negative words are distinguished from the positive by repeating the first consonant ; thus,

⌐ *legible,* ⌐ *illegible ;* ⌐ *moderate,* ⌐ *immoderate ;* ⌐ *necessary,* ⌐ *unnecessary* ⌐ *redeemable,* ⌐ *irredeemable.*

Where the outline for the negative word differs from that written for the positive, repetition of the first consonant is unnecessary ; thus,

⌐ *resolute,* ⌐ *irresolute ;* ⌐ *limited,* ⌐ *illimited.*

Exercise 83

Read, copy, and transcribe

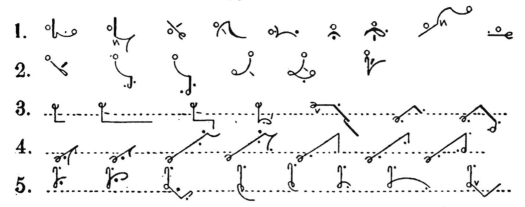

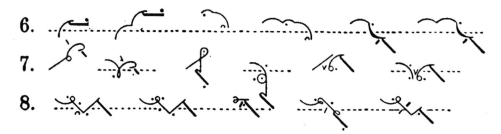

Exercise 84

Write in Shorthand

1. Self-same, self-adjusting, self-satisfied, self-praise, self-protection, self-sacrifice, self-support.
2. Self-condemned, self-complacent, self-conceit, self-congratulation, self-content, self-convicted.
3. Instructress, instruments, instructs, inscriber, inscroll, inscriptive.
4. Inhaler, inheritable, inhibit, inhibition, inhabitation, inhabited.
5. Transplant, transport, transported, transpose, transposition, transmute, transmutation.
6. Legitimate, illegitimate, mortal, immortal, induced, uninduced, rational, irrational, nerved, unnerved, measurable, immeasurable.
7. Limitable, illimitable, relative, irrelative, relevant, irrelevant.
8. Inhuman, inhumanity, inhospitable, inhumanly.

Grammalogs and Contractions

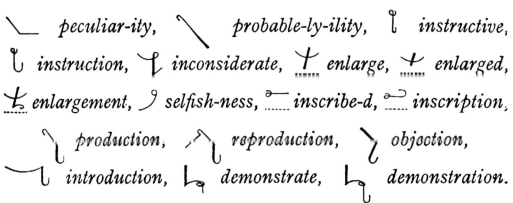

peculiar-ity,   probable-ly-ility,   instructive, instruction,   inconsiderate,   enlarge,   enlarged, enlargement,   selfish-ness,   inscribe-d,   inscription, production,   reproduction,   objection, introduction,   demonstrate,   demonstration.

Exercise 85

Read, copy, and transcribe

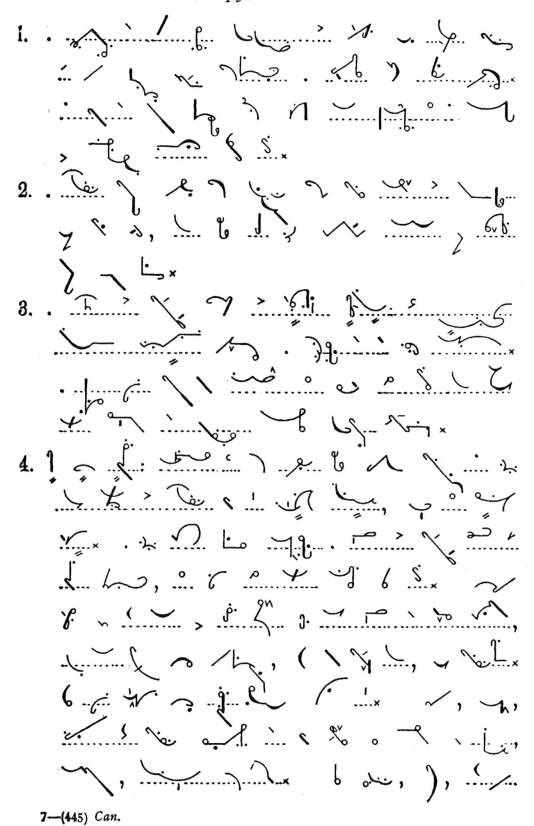

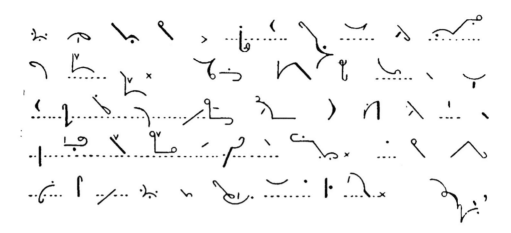

Exercise 86

Write in Shorthand

1. Among-*the* charges preferred against *the* inspector were-*the* following : *that-he-was* exceedingly *selfish and-inconsiderate and-that-he* lacked-*the* self-possession *and* self-control so essential *to-the* proper conduct *of-the* office he held.

2. If-*you*-will grant us *an* interview, *we-shall-be*-pleased *to demonstrate to-your* complete *satisfaction that our* machines will-*do all-that-is* claimed *for-them.*

3. Photographic *reproductions of-the inscriptions* were transmitted *to* scientists *all-over-the* world, *but* only after considerable effort were they *satisfactorily* deciphered.

4. *Mr.* Joseph Manning.

   Dear-Sir :

   Under-the peculiar-circumstances you-mention *in-your* communication *of-the* 15th instant, *we-are*-not at-*all surprised* at-*the* attitude *you have* assumed. *We-do*-not *wish to enlarge* upon *this, but-we-do* take exception *to* condemnation *without* reasonable consideration *of the* explanation *we* offer. *In-all-probability the* unsatisfactory service rendered by-*the* machine *is* due *to*-some slight fault easily remedied. *There-is-*

no *justification for-your* consistent refusal *to*-permit us *to*-make *a* thorough examination *to* determine *the* exact cause *of-the*-trouble. *As a* matter *of* self-protection, if-*the* fault lies *in-the* construction *of-the* machine, *we*-want *to* know *it*. *We-are* confident *of* adjusting-*the* matter *to-your* complete *satisfaction* if-*you*-will permit us *to do*-so.

Very-truly-*yours*,   (137)

Summary

1. The prefix *con-*, *com-* or *cum-*, is indicated by a light dot or by writing two consonants close to each other.

2. The medial sound of *cog-* is represented by disjoining the stroke which follows the syllable.

3. (*a*) A joined or disjoined ___ represents *accom-*.

    (*b*) A joined or disjoined ⌣ represents *intro-*.

    (*c*) A disjoined ⌒ represents *magna-e-i-*.

    (*d*) A disjoined circle represents *self-*. Written in the place of the *con* dot, it represents *self-con-*.

4. A small hook written with the right motion represents *in-* before the circle letters ⌐ ○— ⌀

5. The letter *n* may generally be omitted in the prefix *trans-*.

6. Where necessary a negative word may be distinguished from a positive by repeating the first consonant.

7. When *in-* means *not*, it is always represented by the *n* stroke.

LESSON XVI

56. Suffixes and Word-endings. Where the stroke ⌣ cannot be conveniently employed, the suffix *-ing* is expressed by a light dot, and the plural *-ings* by a light dash ; thus,

⌣⋅ *plotting,* ⌣_ *plottings ;* ⌣⋅ *winning,* ⌣_ *winnings.*

(*a*) *-lity* or *-rity*, preceded by any vowel, is expressed by disjoining the preceding stroke ; thus,

⌐ *durability,* ⌣ *finality,* ⌢ *regularity,* ⊤ *majority.*

Exercise 87

Write in Shorthand

1. Dealing, mutilating, convincing, entertaining, warming, trusting, warning.
2. Playing, irritating, hearing, securing, plotting, frustrating, illustrating.
3. Crediting, ordering, lending, completing, deserving, turning.
4. Cautioning, condensing, posting, mustering, glancing, requesting, renting.
5. Clippings, scrapings, borings, winnings, mornings, sweepings.
6. Acceptability, adaptability, popularity, fatality, futility, vitality.
7. Frivolity, generality, hostility, liberality, illegality, mortality, plurality.

(*b*) *logical·ly* is indicated by a disjoined **/** *j*, as in the words

⌐ *mythological,* ⌣ *biological.*

(c) -*ment* is contracted to ‿ *nt* when the sign ∿ cannot be easily joined, and -*mental-ly-ity* is expressed by a disjoined ∿ ; thus,

⟋∿ *resentment,* ∿∿ *imprisonment,*

⋏∿ *refinement,* ⼂ *instrumental,* ⼃∿ *documental.*

(d) -*ship* is expressed by a joined or disjoined ⟋ *sh,* and -*fulness* and -*lessness* or -*lousness* are respectively expressed by a disjoined ∖₀ and ⌒ ; thus,

∖⟍ *hardship,* ⼂ *citizenship,* ⌐∖₀ *carefulness,*

⌐⌒ *carelessness,* ⼂⌒ *sedulousness.*

(e) -*ward* or -*wart,* and -*yard* are expressed by a half-sized *w* and *y* respectively ; thus,

∖∖ *backward,* ∿⌒ *stalwart,* ∿ *brickyard.*

(f) -*ly* is represented by the stroke *l* (disjoined where necessary) and in some cases by the hooked form ; thus,

⼂ *deeply,* ∿ *smoothly,* ∿ *loosely,* ⟍ *easily,*

⟍ *instantly,* ∿ *friendly.*

Exercise 88

Read, copy, and transcribe

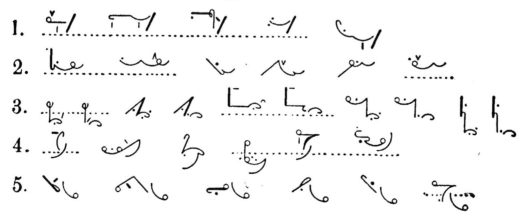

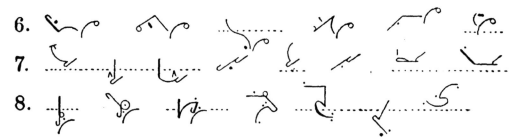

Exercise 89

Write in Shorthand

1. Astrological, ethnological, philological, mineralogical.
2. Imprisonment, commencement, enlistment, accompaniment, preferment, effacement.
3. Supplement, supplemental, experiment, experimental, department, departmental, sacrament, sacramental, fundamental.
4. Directorship, courtship, midship, trusteeship, wardship, editorship.
5. Lawfulness, rightfulness, spitefulness, trustfulness, usefulness.
6. Sleeplessness, tastelessness, friendlessness, lawlessness, zealousness, scrupulousness.
7. Upward, Edward, awkward, *in*ward, rearward, skyward, schoolyard, shipyard.
8. Prudently, stringently, evenly, faintly, rightfully, possibly, physically.

CONTRACTIONS

↳ *nevertheless*,   ⊤ *notwithstanding*,   ∨◠ *perform-ed*,

◠◦ *performs-ance*,   ◡ *efficient-ly-cy*,   ◡ *sufficient-ly-cy*,

↳ *deficient-ly-cy*,   ◡ *proficient-ly-cy*,   ◠◦ *inspect-ed-ion*,

◠◦ *expensive*,   ↳ *distinguish-ed*,   ◠ *relinquish-ed*,

◡ *appointment*,   ◠ *emergency*.

Exercise 90

Read, copy, and transcribe

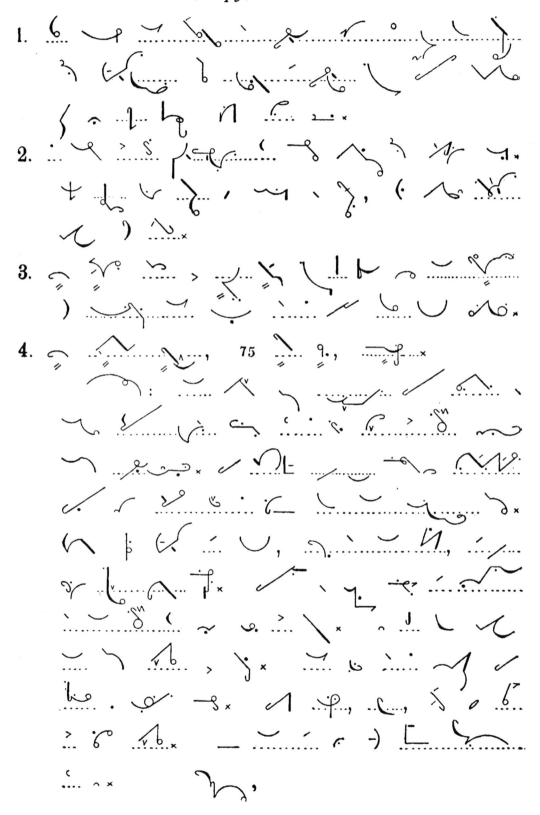

1.

2.

3.

4.   75

Exercise 91

Write in Shorthand

1. *The* Tax Department *has several* vacancies *for* men *who-are proficient in* accounting *and* auditing. They-must also-*be sufficiently* well-versed *in-the Income* Tax Law *to*-recognize attempted evasions *because of* technicalities.

2. *It-was* suggested *that a* minority report *be* submitted opposing-*the* recommendations agreed upon by-*the* majority *of-the members of-the* finance committee.

3. *Notwithstanding-the* speaker's popularity *it* required considerable resourcefulness *on-his* part *to* convince *his* hearers *of-the* feasibility *and practic*ability *of establish*ing *a* motion picture censorship.

4. *Dear Mr.* Winters :

   The Standard Construction Company *of* Winnipeg, Manitoba, *has* consulted us *as-to-the* advisability *of* instituting suit against *you for-the* recovery *of* certain documents, now *in-your* possession, *which-are-the* property *of-our*-clients. *We-have-been* informed *that-you have* refused *to-relinquish them, notwithstanding-the* repeated requests made by *our*-clients. *We* strongly urge-*the* settling *of all* disputes out-*of* court, so-*as-to* avoid *expensive* litigation, *and-we-do*-not entertain-*the* slightest doubt *as-to-the* possibility *of*-such *a* settlement *in-the*-present-instance. *It*-seems self-evident *to* us *that-the* application *of a* little common-sense *on* both sides *ought to*-set matters right *in a very-short* time. Will-*you* kindly let us know *when-we*-may interview *you* regarding-*the*-matter ?

   Very-truly-*yours,*   (139)

SUMMARY

1. A light dot is employed for ‿ and a light dash for ‿ where the stroke form cannot be written easily.

2. (a) *-lity* or *-rity*, preceded by any vowel, is expressed by a disjoined stroke.

    (b) *-logical-ly* is expressed by a disjoined /

    (c) *-ment* is expressed by a joined ‿

    (d) *-mental-ly-ity* is expressed by a disjoined ‿

    e) *-ship* is expressed by a joined or disjoined ⌐

    (f) *-fulness* and *-lessness* or *-lousness* are expressed by a disjoined ↳ and ⌐ respectively.

    (g) *-ward* or *-wart* and *-yard* are expressed by half-length *w* and *y* respectively.

3. The suffix *-ly* is disjoined in some words and in others the termination is expressed by a hooked form.

LESSON XVII

57. Consecutive Vowels. Two consecutive and separately pronounced vowels are expressed by a small angular sign called a *diphone*, as follows—

The sign ⌄ represents a dot vowel followed by any other vowel, and the sign ⌃ represents a dash vowel followed by any other vowel. The first vowel sound in the combination determines the place of the sign ; thus,

⟍ *Sahib,* ⌐⟍ *gaiety,* (*theatre,* ⌐ *drawing,*

⌐⟍ *slower,* ⌄ *brewery,* ⌐ *cruelly.*

(*a*) The angular sign ⌄ is also used to represent the consecutive vowels in the small class of words like

⟍ *Spaniard,* ⌐ *question,* ⌐ *million.*

(*b*) In proper names, where the distinction is necessary, separate vowel signs are employed ; thus,

⌐ *Leah,* ⌐ *Leo.*

Exercise 92

Read, copy, and transcribe

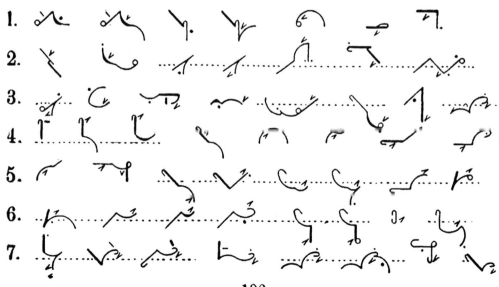

106

Exercise 93

Write in Shorthand

1. Clay, clayey, saying, crayon, sprayer, obeyer, aeroplane, aeronaut.
2. Ideal, gaudier, gaudiest, associate, association, experience, experiences, experienced.
3. Reconciliation, audience, champion, myriad, acquiesce, appropriate, appropriation, creation.
4. Co-operate, co-operation, co-operative, poet, heroic, coercion, co-ordinate, co-ordination.
5. Affluent, bluish, ruinously, wrongdoer, undoing, jewelry, cruelty.
6. Exhaust, exhaustion, digestion, medallion, companion.

58. Medial Use of Semicircle. The use of the right semicircle as an abbreviation for *w* initially with the strokes ⎯ ⎯ ⌢ ⟍ and ⟋ is explained in Lesson 6, paragraph 23. The strokes ⌢ ⟍ ⌒ and ⟍ should be included with them.

The semicircle is used *medially* also as follows—

(*a*) A *left* semicircle represents the combination of *w* and a *dot* vowel, long or short.

(*b*) A *right* semicircle represents the combination of *w* and a *dash* vowel, long or short.

These semicircles are written in the *place* indicated by the vowel following the *w*; thus,

⤳ *mademoiselle,* ⟩ *assuage,* ⟩⤳ *Oswego,* ⟍ *seaward,* ⌢ *misquote,* ⌢ *lamb's-wool.*

Exercise 94

Read, copy, and transcribe

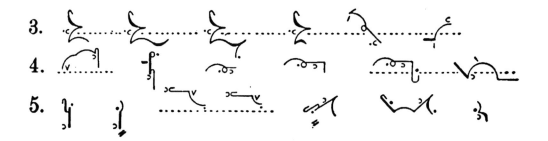

3.
4.
5.

Exercise 95

Write in Shorthand

1. Subsequent, subsequently, Harwell, twelfth, reservoir.
2. Sandwich, twaddle, frequenter, frequenting, unfrequented.
3. Quality, qualification, breakwater, woodwork, stonework.
4. Windward, guesswork, groundwork, *overwork*, *overworked*.

CONTRACTIONS

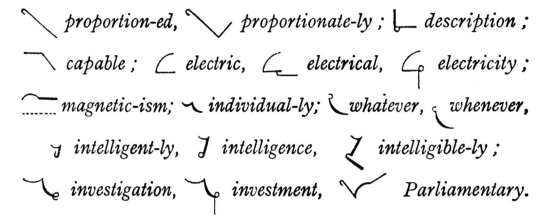

proportion-ed, proportionate-ly ; description ; capable ; electric, electrical, electricity ; magnetic-ism; individual-ly; whatever, whenever, intelligent-ly, intelligence, intelligible-ly ; investigation, investment, Parliamentary.

Exercise 96

Read, copy, and transcribe

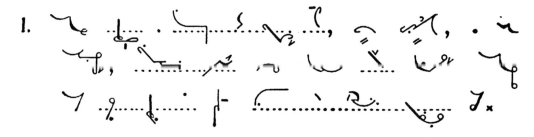

1.

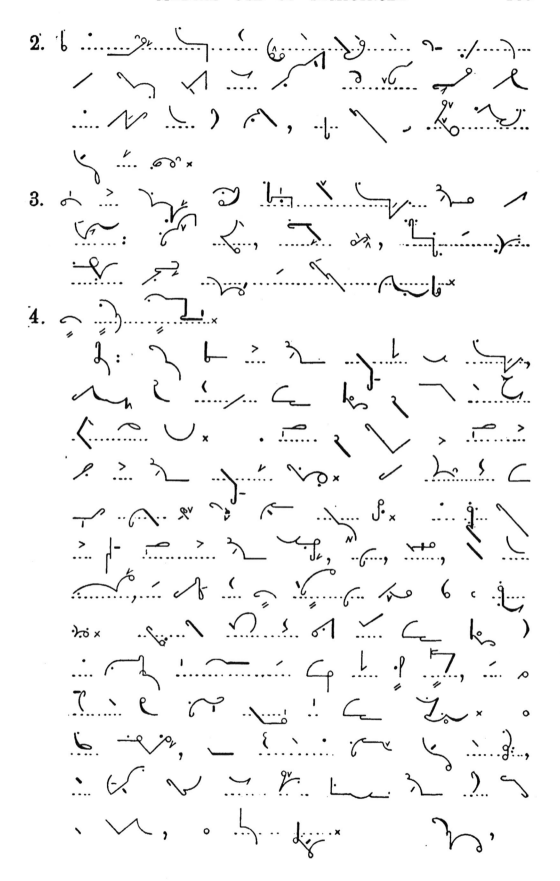

Exercise 97

Write in Shorthand

1. Aerial photography, formerly considered *a* novelty, *is*-now playing *a most-important* part *in-the* affairs *of-the* world.

2. *Although Mr.* Eastwood *was an* experienced *public* speaker, he-*was* frequently interrupted *on-this* occasion by *several in-the* audience *to*-whom *his remarks* were un*intelligible*.

3. *The* findings *of-the* geological survey were discussed by-*the Parliamentary* Committee *which* reported *unanimously in*-favor *of an* appropriation *of* funds *to be* used *for* further surveys *in-the* coal fields.

4. Messrs. Wagstaff *&* Wimple.

Gentlemen :

Frequent reference *to-the* volume *you sent me* last week *has* convinced *me that-you have performed your* task *most efficiently.* It-will add *to-your established* reputation. *The* author *has a peculiar* gift *of description that* arrests *and*-grips *the* reader's attention, *and-I-have*-no-doubt *it*-will appeal *to-the general public. His intelligent* treatment *of-the subject* matter *is* bound *to*-prove highly *instructive as* well *as interesting.* Permit *me to* congratulate *all* concerned upon-*the* splendid work *you have put* forth.

Very-truly-*yours,* (95)

Summary

1. The angular signs ⌐ ⌐ are employed to represent a vowel followed by another vowel.

2. A semicircle is employed medially to represent *w* and a vowel.

LESSON XVIII

59. Figures. Figures *one* to *seven* and the figure *nine* are best represented by shorthand outlines. Other numbers, except round numbers, are expressed by the Arabic numerals. Round numbers are expressed as follows—

⌣ for *hundred* or *hundredth* ; thus, 4 , 400.

(or (for *thousand* ; thus, 5(, 5,000 ; 5 , 500,000.

⌢ for *million* ; thus, 4 , 4,000,000.

\\ for *billion* ; thus, 2\\ , *two billions.*

(for *dollars* ; thus, 15(, $15 ; 250(, $250,000.

Dollars and *cents* may be written thus, 7^{16}, $7.16.

60. Intersections. The practice of intersecting one stroke through another is a most useful aid in the development of speed. The method is applied to the representation of titles of companies or persons and to commonly occurring phrases. Where intersection is not practicable, write one stroke close to another. The following partial list shows how the device may be applied to any special needs of the writer.

P represents *party*—

political party

Conservative party

party question

Pr represents *Professor*—

Professor Jackson

Professor Robertson

Professor of Chemistry

111

B represents *bank—*

⟩⟨ bank rate

⟨ city bank

central bank

T represents *attention—*

early attention

necessary attention

my attention has been called

D represents *department—*

science department

home department

wireless department

electrical department

foreign department

school department

department of economics

J represents *Journal—*

Bankers' Journal

Engineering Journal

Journal of Commerce

K represents *company* and other words—

rubber company

Steel & Iron Company

Cab Co.

Town Council

capital punishment

share capital

Captain Thomson

ship's captain

Kr represents *Colonel* and *Corporation—*

Colonel Alexander

Colonel Johnson

public corporation

G represents *Government—*

Government official

French Government

British Government

F represents *form—*

necessary form

as a matter of form

form of the report

V represents *valuation—*

    low valuation

    high valuation

    valuation of the factory

Th represents *authority* or *month—*

    local authority

    sanitary authority

    for a month

    six months ago

S represents *society—*

    dramatic society

    Electrical Society

    society of musicians

M represents *mark* or *Major—*

    auditor's mark

    water mark

    high-water mark

    Major Locker

    Major Johnson

N represents *national—*

    national defence

    national affairs

    national dividends

R (down) represents *arrange-d-ment—*

    I shall arrange the matter

    please make arrangements

    we have arranged

R (up) represents *railway, railroad,* or *require-d-ment—*

    State railways

    railway commission

    Metropolitan Railway

    inter-urban railroads

    railroad facilities

    you may require

    will be required

    your requirements

Exercise 98

Read, copy, and transcribe

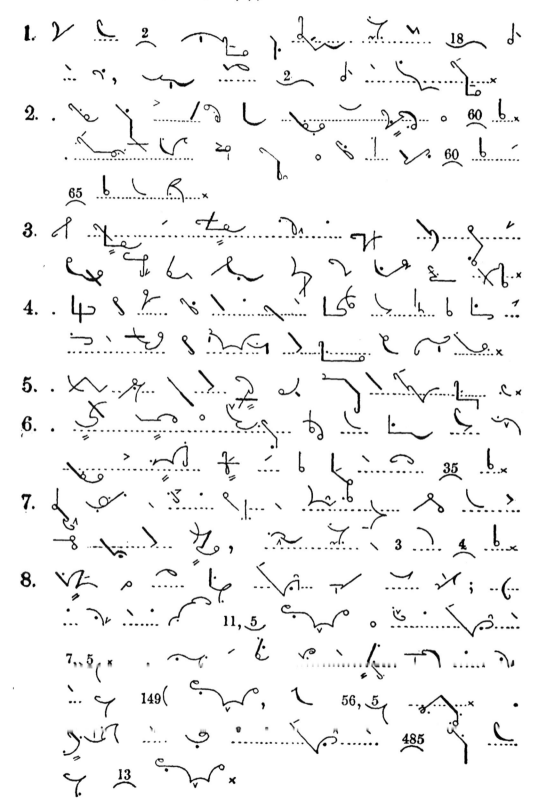

Exercise 99

Write in Shorthand

1. *Over two* hundred million dollars *is* invested *in-the* citrus industry *in* California, *with more*-than 150,000 persons directly or indirectly supported by *it*.

2. *It-is* estimated *that* at-*the* present-time *there-is a* total *of* $5,250,000,000 foreign capital invested *in* Canada. *Of-this the* United-States *has-been responsible for* $2,500,000,000 *according-to-the* same estimate.

3. Seven thousand stockholders *of-the General* Cigar Company will share *in-the* dividends just declared by directors. *The* dividends *are* $40,000 *to-the* preferred *and* $27,000,000 *to-the* common stockholders.

4. *The* " Journal *of* Commerce " *for-the* current month *publishes an* article *on-the* proposed merger *of*-several *of-the* leading steel-*and*-iron companies *in-this*-country.

5. *This* article *calls particular* attention *to-the* fact *that-the government* officials *have* sanctioned *the* merger upon-*the* recommendation *of-the* Inter-Province Commerce department.

6. *Immediately* before ministerial elections *are* held, *the* various political parties pay special attention *to-the* national affairs *in-which-the general public* displays un*usual* *interest*.

CONTRACTIONS

↘ *bankruptcy ;* ‾○‾ *cross-examine-d-ation ;* ↗ *England,*

↗ *English ;* ⌐ *enthusiastic-iasm ;* ↘ *familiar-ity,*

↘ *familiarize ;* ↙ *inconvenient-ce ;* ‾ *incorporated ;*

↘ *indispensable-ly ;* ⌒‾ *mortgage-d ;* ‾⌒ *neglect-ed,*

negligence ;   *legislative,*   *legislature ;*   *organizer ;*   *preliminary ;*   *reform-ed ;*   *universe ;*   *prospectus.*

Exercise 100

Read, copy, and transcribe

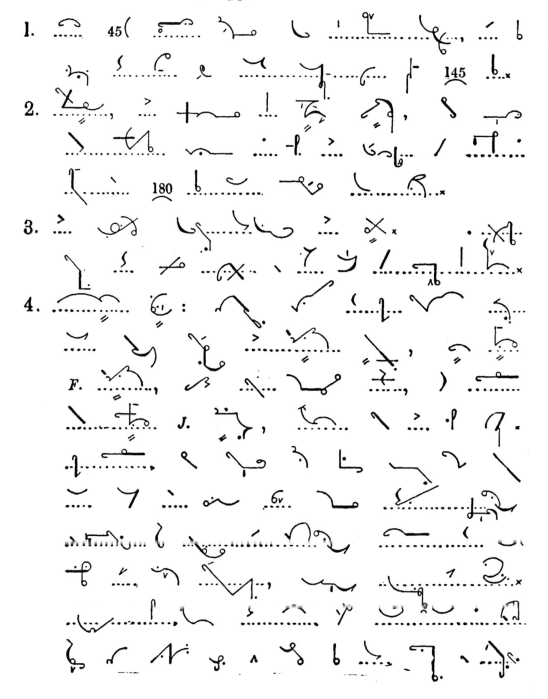

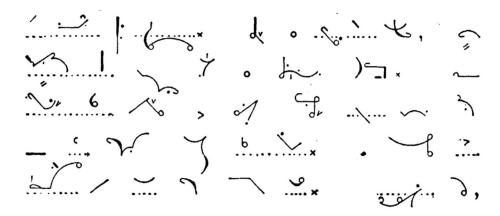

Exercise 101

Write in Shorthand

1. After *all-the* necessary details *had-been* arranged, Capt. Thompson *and* Col. Bender, *two of-the-most* daring aviators *in-the government* service, set out *on-their* trans-continental flight, determined *to* shatter *all* previous records.

2. *The* New York Central Railroad placed *a very* high rental *valuation on-the* property *and-the* equipment *which-it-has* turned *over to-the* postal authorities.

3. *All* party lines were eliminated *during-the* recent discussions *in* Parliament *on-the* question *of* national defence *and-the* necessary appropriations *for-its* requirements were quickly voted.

4. My-*dear*-Sir :

Evidently, investors *are very*-much alike *all-over-the* world. They pay *too*-little attention *and*-thought *to-the* essential requirement *of* safety *when* investing *their* funds. *In-England*, France *and-several* other European countries, *as* well *as in* Canada *and-the* United-States, millions *of* dollars *are* lost annually by-those-*who-can* least afford *it, because of-the* lure *of* high returns *and* quick profits. They *neglect to*-make *a careful* study *of-the* enterprises *in-which-their* money *is* invested *and-the* inevitable result *of-this negligence is-the* total loss *of* hard-earned savings. Officials, *however,* *are* striving *to* safe*guard* these earnings by-means-*of* *legislative reforms.* They hope *to* enact laws providing *for* heavy fines *and*-prison terms *for-those* promoters *of* stock issues *who*-make misleading statements *in-the prospectus* they *put* forth. *In* addition, *the* Treasury Department *has* planned *a* campaign *of* education whereby-*the* man or woman *with* surplus funds will-*be* taught *to*-choose *investments more intelligently.* Address *your financial* inquiries *to* Savings Banks, *the* Federal Reserve Bank, or-*the* Treasury Department, *and*-they-will gladly *give-you-the information you* seek.

Very-truly-*yours,*   (197)

SUMMARY

1. Intersection is a brief method of indicating commonly occurring titles, phrases, etc. The principle of intersection may be adapted as required to suit special cases.

2. The figures *one* to *seven* and *nine* should be expressed in shorthand. The strokes ⌣ *n,* (*th,* ⌢ *m* are used to express *hundred, thousand* and *million* respectively. The stroke \ *b* is employed for *billion,* ⌊ *ds* for *dollars.*

LESSON XIX

61. Proper Names, etc. Proper names, initials, **and** such abbreviations as C.O.D., f.o.b., and O.K. are **best** written in longhand.

62. Compound Words. Compounds of *here*, *there*, *where*, etc., are written as follows—

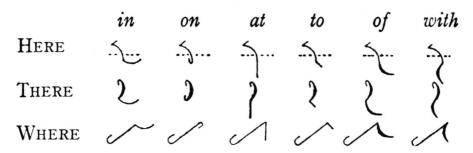

	in	*on*	*at*	*to*	*of*	*with*
HERE						
THERE						
WHERE						

63. Advanced Phrasing. Many of the ordinary abbreviating devices are employed for more advanced phrases. The circle *s* is used to express *us* in a phrase like *please let us know*. The circle *sw* is used for *as we* in a phrase like *as we know*. The circle for *ss* is used **to** express the two *s*'s in a phrase like *this city*. Hook *f* or *v* represents the words *have* or *of* in such phrases as—

who have been, *ought to have been,* *rate of interest.*

Sometimes a letter or a syllable is omitted, as—

in this (m)anner, *I have (con)cluded,* *I will (con)sider.*

There are many instances in which one or more words may be omitted without affecting the legibility of the phrase ; thus,

119

again (and) again,   *there must (have) been,*   *fact (of the) matter,*   *more (or) less.*

Colloquial phrases such as *you've,* *we've,* *haven't,* *wasn't,* *isn't,* *can't,* are written as here shown.

The following illustrations will suggest others.

of us			Tuesday evening
to us			at all events
please let us know			able to make
as we can			as if it were
as we think			you are not
as we shall			you were not
as well as possible			we would
as soon as possible			at any rate
it is said			from time to time
in this city			I am sure there is
of this statement			I have been there
Wednesday next			in which there is
in our view			by some other means
it appears			my dear sir
by all means			my dear madam
it is only necessary			we have received
more than			most probable
longer than			in fact
I had been			in this manner
those who have been			in the same manner
Thursday afternoon			one another

I hope

on the contrary

satisfactory conclusion

which will be considered

shall be taken into consideration

at a loss

to a great extent

all the way

into the matter

on the subject

under the circumstances

our own

in accordance with

in consequence of

in respect of

in respect to

on the part of

out of place

face to face

from first to last

with regard to

with respect to

we shall be glad to know

more and more

bear in mind

borne in mind

fact of the matter

two or three

three or four

six or seven

in reply

in reply to your letter

I regret

I regard

I am instructed

I am instructed to inform you

I am requested to inform you

referring to our letter

referring to your letter

referring to your favor

registered letter

very truly yours

yours very truly

respectfully yours

yours respectfully

yours sincerely

deliver immediately

please forward

lowest terms

best quality

balance sheet

account sales

best thanks

best finish

best possible

best of my ability

best of my recollec-
tion

make an appointment

additional cost

additional expense

Exercise 102

Read, copy, and transcribe

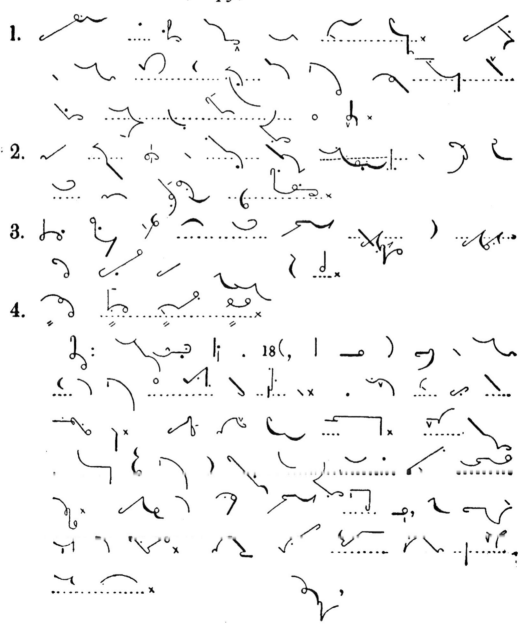

Exercise 103

Write in Shorthand

1. *The* receipt *of-your* check *is* hereby *acknowledged. We*-assure-*you that our* service *in-the* future will-*be as satisfactory to-you as-it-has-been* heretofore.

2. *We*-received *your* communication *and immediately* looked *into-the*-matter *therein* mentioned. *There-is*-no-doubt *that a satisfactory*-conclusion *can-be* reached, *and-we*-hope *to-be*-able-*to* make-*the* necessary arrangements *without any* additional-expense *to-you.*

3. *The* fact-*of-the*-matter *is that-you-are*-not well-*informed on-the-subject.* Upon *investigation, it*-appears-*that* not-only *the* medical-societies *but-the* federal authorities *as*-well, *have* at-*all*-times *been* ready *and*-anxious *to* co-operate *in* stamping out-*the* drug evil.

4. Messrs. Wright *&* Dawson.

   Dear-Sirs :

   We-thank-you for-the communication *we-have*-just-received *from-you under-the* date *of* June 9. *Our* new price-list *and* samples *are being* forwarded *to-you as you* requested. *We*-regret-*the* delay *in* attending *to-this*-matter, *but* pressure *of* work *in*-connection-*with several* big contracts *for-the* War-Office *has* rendered *it more*-or-less *impossible for*-us *to*-go *into-the* question earlier. If-*you* decide *to*-place *an* order *with*-us, *we-shall-be* ready *to*-make *delivery any*-time after Wednesday-*next.*

   Very-truly-*yours,*   (100)

CONTRACTIONS

⤳ *govern-ed,* ⤳ *government ;* ⤳ *manufacture-d,* ⤳ *manufacturer ;* ⌐ *exchange-d ;* ⤳ *independent-ly-ce ;* ⤳ *sensible-ly-ility ;* ⌐ *maximum ;* ⤳ *minimum ;* ⤳ *universal ;* ⤳ *mechanical-ly.*

Exercise 104

Read, copy, and transcribe

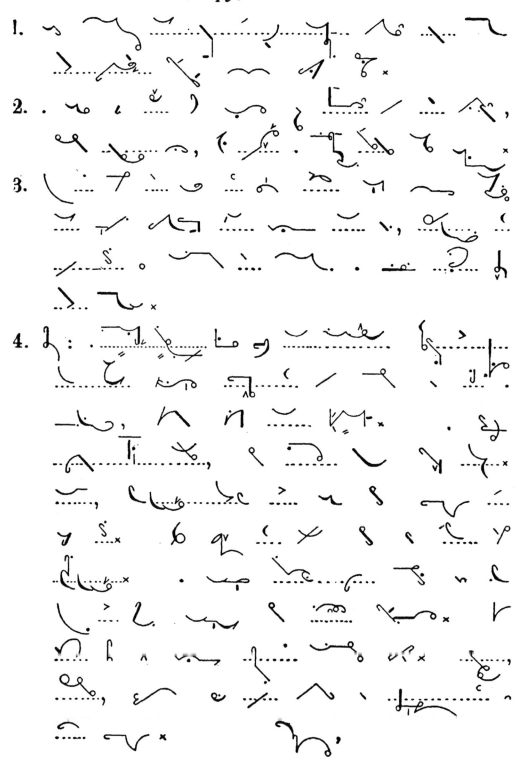

Exercise 105

Write in Shorthand

1. *We-have*-just-received-*the certificate of* incorporation *and it-is* just-possible *that-the*-directors will meet *next*-week to-perfect *their organization.*

2. *Mr.* Henry Wheelock incurred-*the* displeasure *of-his* employer *and was discharged because-he* permitted un*satisfactory* business relationships *to* continue *for*-some-time.

3. Stock-brokers were astonished *to*-receive *an* order *from-the* Advisory Council *of-the* Stock-*Exchange* indicating-*the character of-the* announcements *to be*-made *in-their* newspaper *adverti*sing.

4. *Gentlemen :*

   As-soon-*as-it-is* convenient *for-you to-do*-so, please-make-*an-appointment to-call* at *our* offices *for-the* purpose *of* discussing-*the* advisability *of*-bringing suit against *the* Standard Construction Company *for* infringements *on-your* patents. *We-have* gone *into-the*-matter *from* every point-*of*-view *and-have*-concluded *that-you have an* excellent case against *them in*-spite-*of any* defence they-might advance. *In*-fact, *we-can* see *but* one out*come to-the* litigation proceedings, even if-*it should-be* necessary *to*-go *to*-trial. *Under-the*-circumstances, *we* confidently *expect an* offer *to* compromise *and* settle *as*-soon-*as-we* notify *them of-our* intention *to*-take-*the*-matter *to*-court. *We-would* appreciate *an* early-reply *from-you* indicating *your* purpose *in-this*-matter.

   Very-truly-*yours,* (137)

SUMMARY

1. In advanced phrasing the following abbreviations are employed—

 (*a*) Circle *s* for *us*.

 (*b*) *Sw* circle for *as we*.

 (*c*) *SS* circle for two *s's* in separate words.

 (*d*) Hook *f* or *v* for *of, have*.

2. Phrases are frequently abbreviated by the omission of a letter, a syllable, or a word.

LESSON XX

64. Distinguishing Vowels. The consonantal structure of English words is such that the shorthand outlines for them, when left unvocalized, generally suggest the words. Nevertheless, the rules of Isaac Pitman Shorthand have been so devised that in many instances vowels are indicated without actually writing the vowel-sign. In practice, therefore, vocalization is required only to a very limited extent. Where, however, a necessary distinguishing vowel is not indicated either by position or by the shorthand outline, the vowel-sign should be inserted ; thus,

apposite, *opposite ;* *absolute,* *obsolete ;* *adapt,* *adopt ;* *obey,* *echo.*

65. Distinguishing Outlines. The wealth of alternative forms provided in the system enables the shorthand writer to make the necessary distinction between different words containing the same consonants and thus avoid hesitation in the transcription of his notes. The following list will suggest to the student the lines upon which other pairs of words may be distinguished.

petrify	property	prosecute
putrefy	propriety	persecute
passionate	appropriation	prosecution
patient	preparation	persecution
purpose	proffer	debtor
propose	prefer	editor
appropriate	provide	differ
purport	pervade	defer

127

courage	pure	comparative
carriage	poor	operative
factor	temperate	portend
factory	tempered	pretend
favored	goodness	person
favorite	guidance	parson
valuable	greatly	parcel
available	gradually	parasol
considerate	evidence	breath
considered	confidence	birth, berth
impassioned	station	burial
impatient	situation	endless
unavoidable	patron	needless
inevitable	pattern	trifle
learned	proper	trivial
learned	prepare	travel
regard	protect	indefinite
regret	product	undefined

Exercise 106

Read, copy, and transcribe

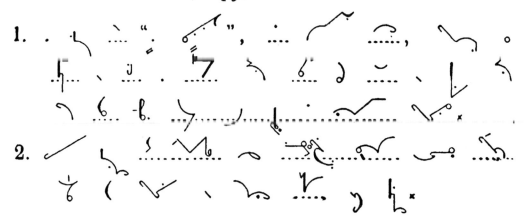

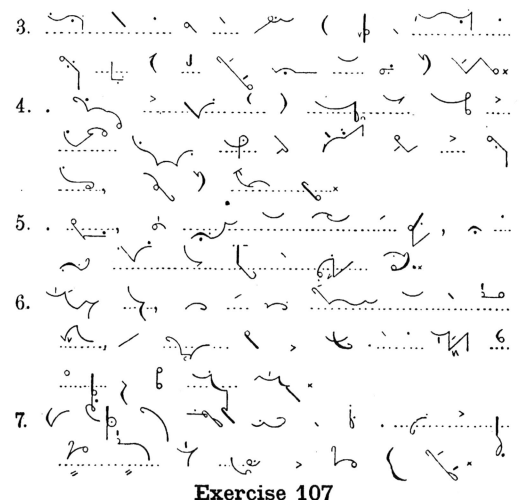

Exercise 107

Write in Shorthand

(The words having distinguishing outlines are printed in small capitals.)

1. *The establishment of a* bureau *for-the* distribution *of information* regarding *commercial* conditions *on-the* continent *is a* VITAL need, *and-we-*REGRET-*the* delay *which-is* proving so FATAL *to-our* progress *in-this* connection.

2. *The* ADVERSE decision handed down *in-the* DIVORCE proceedings *was* entirely un*expected and* proved bitterly disappointing *to-the* AUDITOR.

3. *The* ingenious inventor LABORED hard *for-many-years* before he-*was* finally successful *in* devising *an* ELABORATE *but a most efficient* system *of electrical* signalling *for-the* railroads.

9—(445) *Can.*

4. *As* EVIDENCE *of-his* complete CONFIDENCE *in-his* ward, *the* GUARDIAN recommended *that-the* latter *be given* full control *over his own* PROPERTY.

5. *Although-the* duties *of-the* secretary were clearly defined, definite proof *was* presented *of-his negligence and carelessness in performing them.*

6. *To-*PROTECT *ourselves* against mis*representation of-our* PRODUCTS by *our* competitors, PROPER steps *have-been* taken *to* PREPARE *for our* PATRONS *a* statement explaining *in* detail each *of-the* PATTERNS *we manufacture.*

7. *It-was very* CONSIDERATE *of-you to-*send-us *all-the information* AVAILABLE *on-the-subject. We-have* CONSIDERED *it carefully and-*find *that-it-*will-be extremely VALUABLE *to-*us.

SUMMARY

1. The necessary distinguishing vowel-sign should be inserted in outlines where such vowel is not indicated either by position or by the shorthand form.

2. Words of similar consonantal structure, but of different meaning, may be distinguished where necessary by a difference of outline.

66. **Classified Contractions.** Certain classes of words are contracted by the omission of one or more consonants, or of a syllable, as indicated in the following illustrations :

OMISSION OF N.

passenger,   contingency,   danger,   assignment, entertainment.

OMISSION OF R.

administrate, *administration,* *administrative,*

manuscript, *remonstrate.*

OMISSION OF THE SYLLABLE -ECT.

prospect, *object-ed,* *suspect-ed,* *imperfect-ion-ly.*

OMISSION OF K BEFORE -SHUN.

obstruction, *destruction.*

OMISSION OF KT BEFORE -IVE.

productive, *objective,* *respective,* *irrespective.*

In several instances the same outlines are employed for the derivative as well as the primitive word ; thus,

expected (from *expect*),

respected (from *respect*).

In other instances the derivative is formed by an addition to the contracted outline for the root word ; thus,

enlargement (from *enlarge*), *objectionable* (from *objection*), *publicly* (from *public*), *disorganize* (from *organize*).

There are a few other contracted forms written in accordance with these *abbreviating principles*. These, together with other useful contractions, are to be found in the " *Additional Contractions* " at the end of the book.

Exercise 108

Read, copy, and transcribe

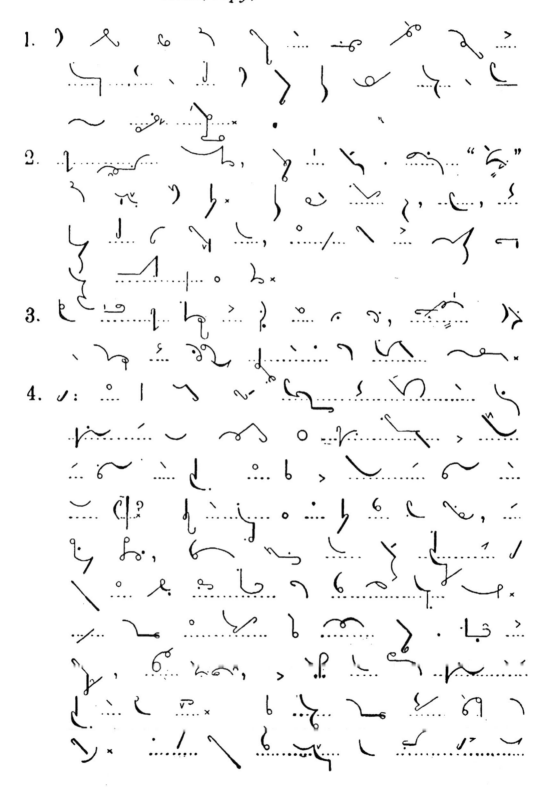

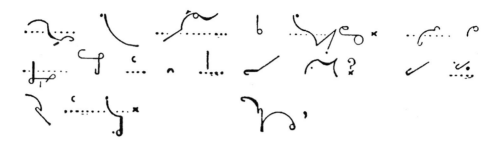

Exercise 109

Write in Shorthand

1. *There-is* every *prospect that-the imperfection* will-*be* discovered. *Our* patrons will undoubtedly *object to-it,* *and-we-shall-be suspected of very* sharp *practice in-the*-matter.

2. *In administrative* circles *it-was* freely predicted *that-the appointment of* Capt. Paul Johnson *would-be*-made, *irrespective of-the objections that-had-been* raised.

3. *Inasmuch-as* a *destruction of*-property values *is sure to*-result if-*the* contemplated health resort *is* built, residents *in-the immediate* vicinity *of* Lakeview Manor *are* determined *to*-place every legal *obstruction that can-be* invoked *in-the* path *of-the* builders.

4. *Dear*-Sir :

   As a sensible executive interested in-the efficient administration of-your business, *you have* undoubtedly *given much* time *and*-thought *to-the* problem *of-the* details *of* office routine. *You* want *to be* absolutely certain *that-you-are*-not using obsolete machinery *and* systems *in-your establishment, for-there-is*-no *great*er detriment *to* successful accomplishment than *an imperfect organization,* wherever-*the imperfection* may exist.

You want *the* best. *Therefore, we* earnestly urge *you to* use *the* enclosed ticket *and* examine *the* world's leading business appliances *and efficiency*-promoting devices *and* systems. Experts will gladly explain *to-you and* make-*you familiar with-the* latest *and most* approved inventions *for* effecting practical economy *in* office, store *and*-factory, *irrespective of* size.

An afternoon or evening at-*the* exposition *is indispensable to-you and* will-*be productive of more* benefit than *several* weeks spent *in-the* ordinary manner *of* investigating time *and* labor-saving devices *and* methods.

Respectfully-yours,   (160)

READING AND DICTATION PRACTICE

The method of counting the words in the following letters and articles is that used by the Contest Committee of the National Shorthand Reporters' Association. Compound words are counted according to the number of single words in the compound. Figures are counted as read. 24' 3" is read twenty-four feet three inches, and is consequently counted as five words; $245.50 is read two hundred forty-five dollars and fifty cents and counted as eight words. Each initial in a proper name is counted as one word. The total number of words is given at the end of each letter or article.

1

(46)

2

(46)

3

(38)

4

(49)

5

[Shorthand outlines] (51)

6

[Shorthand outlines] (50)

7

11(*[Shorthand outlines]*) (53)

8

[Shorthand outlines] "..." J. A. "..." (57)

9

[Shorthand outlines] (48)

10

(shorthand symbols)

(60)

11

(shorthand symbols)

(72)

12

(shorthand symbols)

(62)

13

(shorthand symbols)

(60)

14

[shorthand outlines] 50 *[shorthand outlines]*

(70)

15

[shorthand outlines] 86 *[shorthand outlines]*

T.W. *[shorthand outlines]*

(71)

16

[shorthand outlines]

(74)

17

[shorthand outlines]

(80)

18

(shorthand outlines) 10 ...

(78)

19

(shorthand outlines)

(79)

20

(shorthand outlines)

(80)

21

(shorthand outlines)

(80)

22

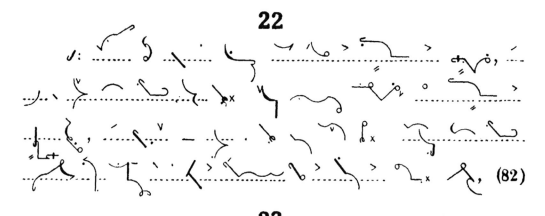

(82)

23

18(

(83)

24

c.o.d.,

(85)

25

F. J. 410

(64)

26

(99)

27

(112)

28

(89)

29

[Pitman shorthand outlines]

(82)

30

[Pitman shorthand outlines]

(92)

31

[Pitman shorthand outlines]

(95)

32

(98)

33

(106)

34

(102)

35

(shorthand outlines)

(103)

36

(shorthand outlines)

(106)

37

(shorthand outlines)

(106)

38

[shorthand outlines]

(107)

39

[shorthand outlines]

(112)

40

[shorthand outlines] 14 *[shorthand]*

3^{15} *[shorthand]* f.o.b. *[shorthand]*

3^{6} *[shorthand]*

(119)

41

(shorthand outlines) (115)

42

(shorthand outlines) (115)

43

(shorthand outlines) (99)

44

(126)

45

(129)

46

[Shorthand outlines] P.B.

7112

13

7110

(145)

47

54

48

(138)

48

[shorthand outlines] 44⁴⁵

(143)

49

(142)

50

(shorthand outlines)

(151)

51

(shorthand outlines)

(143)

52

(shorthand outlines)

f.o.b.

25 45 2⁹⁰ 40 3

(168)

53

(shorthand outlines)

(138)

54

(172)

55

(175)

56

(183)

Freedom

(78)

Work

(79)

Obstacles

(148)

Real Men

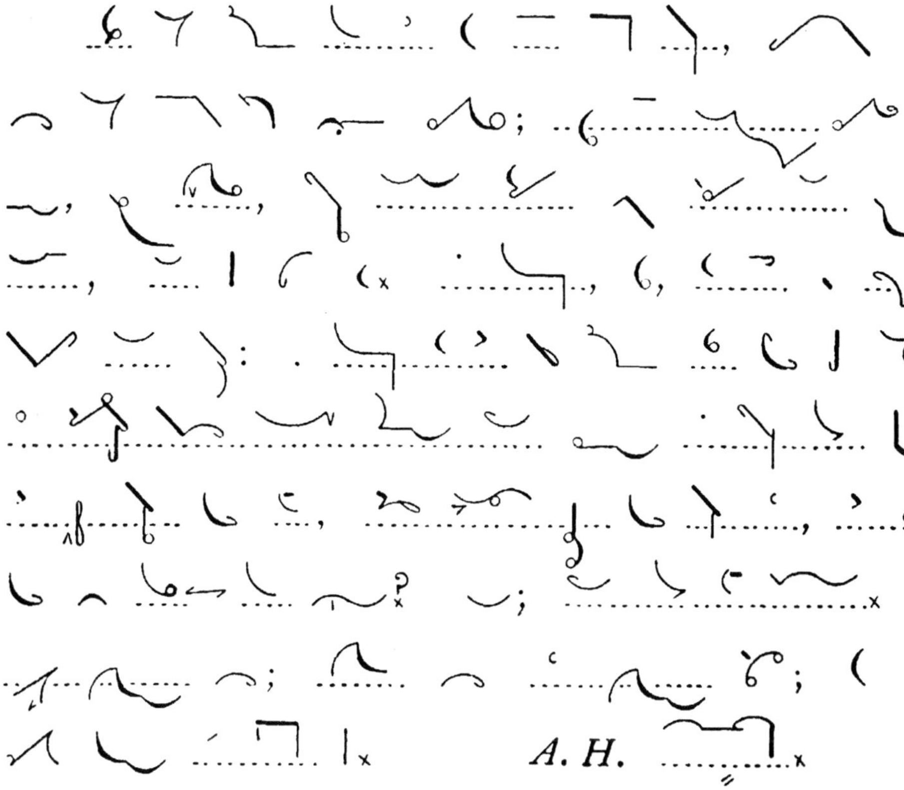

[shorthand content]

A. H. (150)

National Ideals

[shorthand content]

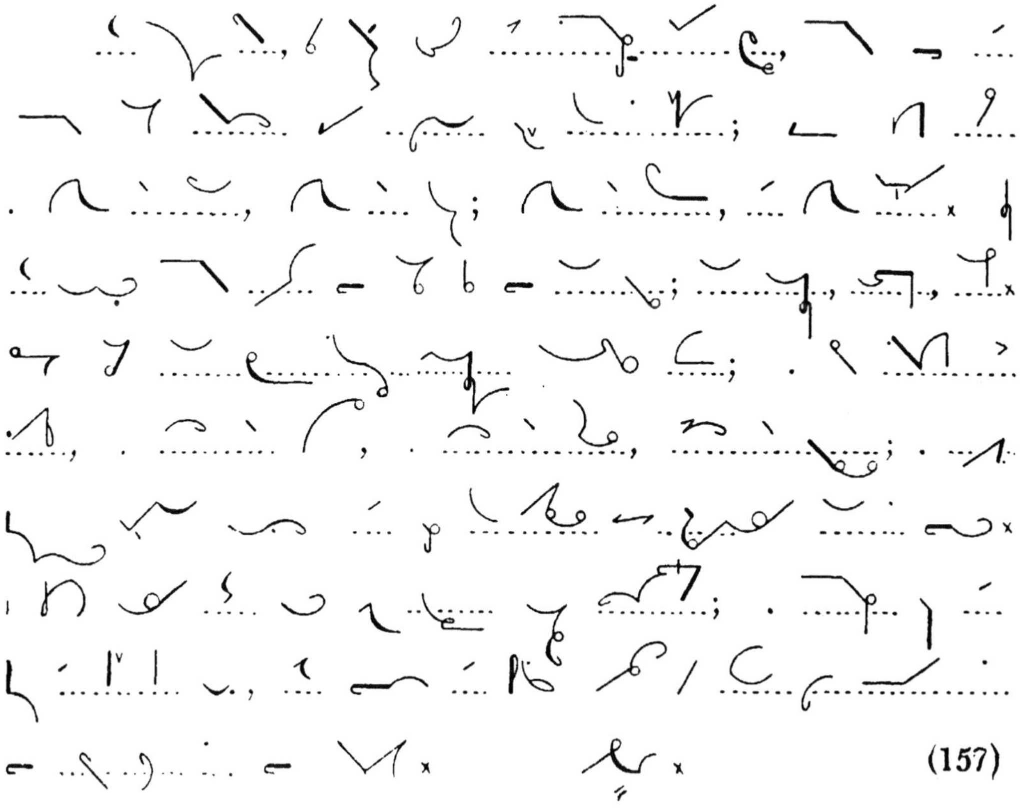

(157)

Hydro-Electric Power

(182)

Municipal Government

(167)

Banking

(shorthand outline)

(210)

Concentration

(shorthand outline)

(134)

British Columbia

(178)

Advertising

(166)

Of Studies

[shorthand]

(164)

Work and Play

[shorthand]

(202)

The Development of the Human Body

Tact

(shorthand outlines)

(322)

The Night Hawk

Central Filing

(298)

Singleness of Purpose

[shorthand content]

(323)

The Management of a Corporation

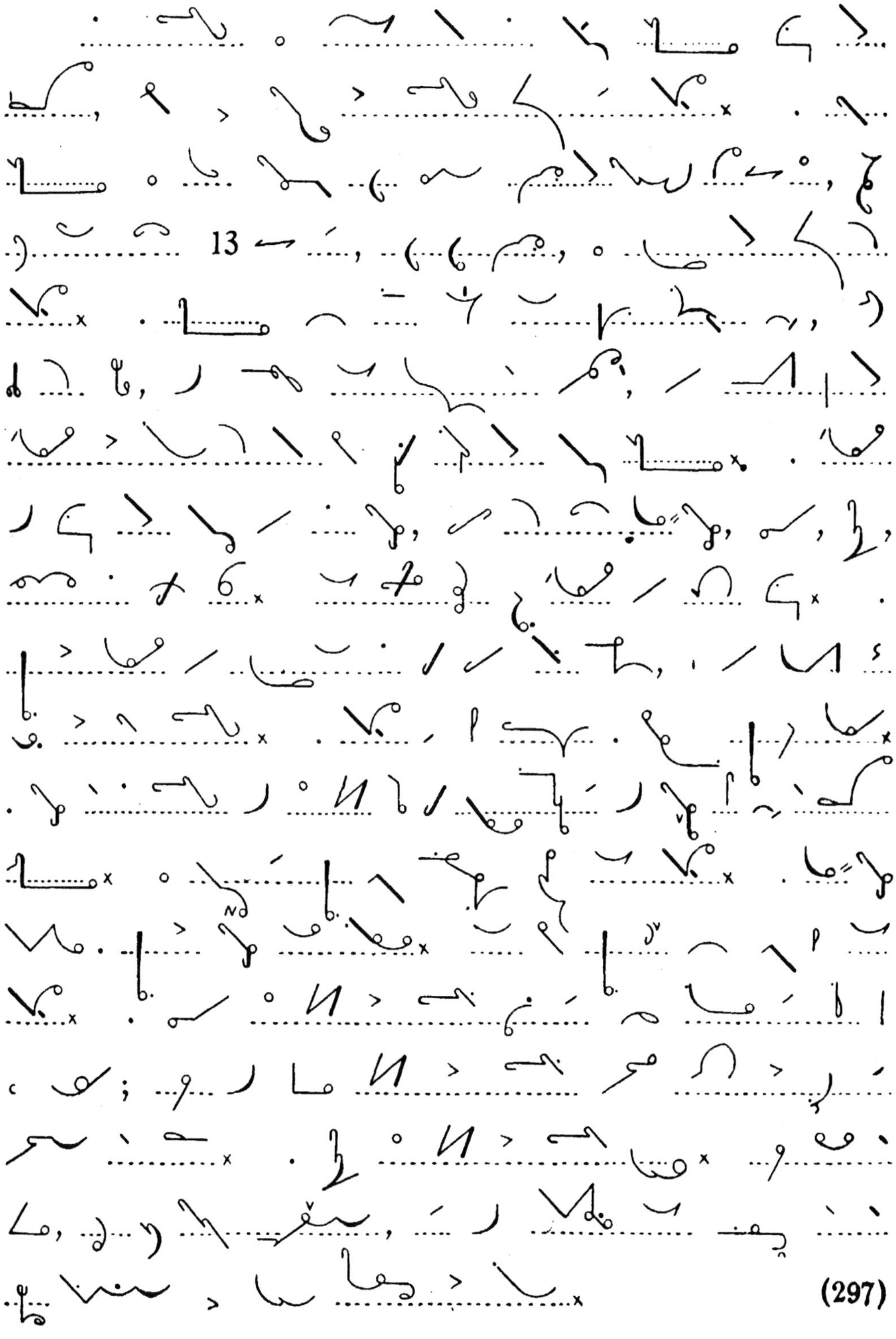

[Shorthand content]

(297)

Economics

Habits of Work

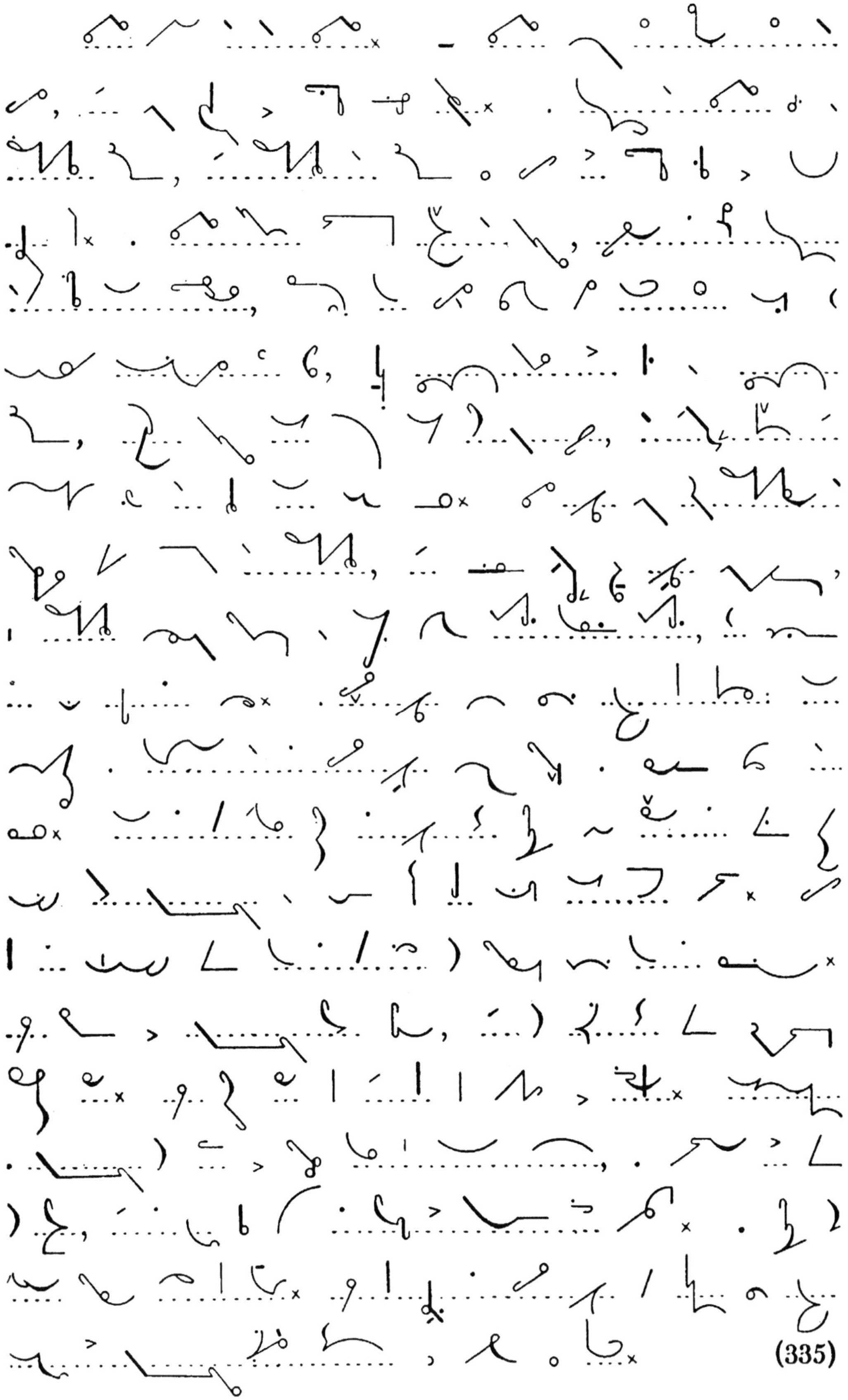

(335)

Some Hints of Business Good Manners

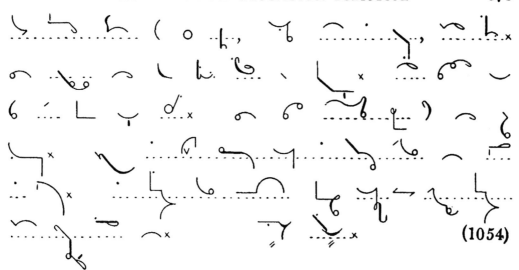

(1054)

PHRASES IN COMMON USE

as it were

brought forward

on either hand

on either side

on the other hand

in this statement

at first cost

it can only be

any longer than

no longer than

rather than

I have been informed

rate of interest

state of affairs

state of business

into effect

at all times

medical association

traders' association

merchants' association

at some time

at the same time

some time ago

we think there is

how can there be

I hope there will be

I shall be there

we know there is not

in other words

in order

in order that

in order to

in order to know

I have received

last week

this week

next week

last month

last year

this month

telegraph office

worth while

is it worth while

in like manner

as far as possible

as much as possible

if it were possible

between them

towards one another

and the contrary

as a rule

in a few days

in a great measure

in such a manner as

all over the world

at the present day

at the present time

by the way

for the first time

in the first instance

in the first place

in the second place

on the one hand

what is the matter with them

as a matter of course

as a matter of fact

as a matter of form

necessary consequence of

I expect to receive

in regard to

having regard to

in reference to

with reference to

in relation to

with relation to

with respect to

it appears to have been

I regret to state

I regret to say

again and again

deeper and deeper

faster and faster

less and less

more or less

north and south

east and west

over and over again

side by side

all parts of the world

facts of the case

for the purpose of

out of the question

one or two

two or three

three or four

six or seven

sooner or later

in accordance with

in accordance with the

in connection with the

additional expense

at your earliest convenience

best of my ability

best of our ability

best of their ability

best of your ability

bill of lading

board of directors

passenger train

director's report

early convenience

I am in receipt of your letter

postal order

referring to our invoice

referring to our letter

referring to your letter

referring to yours

we beg to quote you

House of Representatives

Houses of Parliament

Assembly Chamber

City Council

Council of the City of

Commission Government

Chamber of Commerce

Board of Education

District Attorney

Senate Chamber

President of the United States

Party Leader

Conservative Party

Liberal Party

Prohibition Party

Socialist Party

Labor Party

Federal Government

ProvincialGovernment

In the Assembly

Court of Claims

Postmaster-General

Prime Minister

tax payers

Secretary of State

Secretary of the Interior

Secretary of the Treasury

life insurance

Insurance Co.

Royal Trust Co.

fire insurance

free on board (f.o.b.)

Canadian Pacific (C.P.R.) Railway

Canadian National Railways

Pennsylvania Railroad

Dominion Express Co.

Canadian Express Co.

Articles of Association

counsel for the defence

counsel for the plaintiff

Court of Appeals

Canadian Customs Duties

GRAMMALOGS AND CONTRACTIONS

Arranged in the order in which they are given in the preceding pages

LESSON I. a *or* an, . the, all, too *or* two, of, to, on, but, (*up*) and, (*up*) should, (*down*) awe, aught, *or* ought, who, put, be, to be, it.

LESSON II. had, do, different *or* difference, much, which, large, can, come, go, give *or* given, for, have, thank *or* thanked, think, as *or* has, is *or* his.

LESSON III. though, them, was, whose, shall, wish, usual-ly, me, him, in *or* any, own, language *or* owing, thing, young, your, year, we.

LESSON IV. are, our *or* hour, that, without, sent, quite, could, most, influence, influenced, next, first, myself, himself.

LESSON V. because, itself, those, this, thus, several, themselves, ourselves, influences, anything, something, nothing, as is, is as.

175

LESSON VI. how, why, with, when, what, would, beyond, you, acknowledge, knowledge, acknowledged, O, Oh *or* owe, he.

LESSON VII. special *or* specially, speak, dollar, dollars, establish-ed-ment, expect-ed, unexpected, altogether, together, insurance, January, February, November *or* never, yesterday, regular, irregular.

LESSON VIII. people, belief-ve-d, tell, till, deliver-ed-y, largely, call, equal-ly, truth, doctor, dear, during, principal-le-ly, liberty, member *or* remember-ed, number-ed, larger, care, surprise, surprised.

LESSON IX. over, however, valuation, their *or* there, therefore, from, very, sure, pleasure, more *or* remark-ed, remarkable-y, Mr. *or* mere, nor, near.

LESSON X. been, general-ly, within, southern, northern, opinion, balance, deliverance, signify-led-ficant, significance, behalf, advantage, difficult, difficulty.

LESSON XI. ⟍ public-sh-ed, ⟍ publication, ⟍ subject-ed, ⟍ subjective, ⟍ subjection, ⌐ signification, ⟍ subscribe-d, ⟍ subscription, ⌐ inform-ed, ⌐ informer, ⌐ information, ⋀ represent-ed, ⋀ representative, ⋀ representation, ∫ satisfaction, ∫ satisfactory, ⟍ organization, ⟍ organize-d, ∫ generalization, ∫ justification, ⋀ responsible-ility, ⟍ irresponsible-ility, ∫ circumstance, ∫ circumstances, ⟍ circumstantial.

LESSON XII. ⌐ important-ce, ⌐ improve-d-ment, ⌐ impossible, ⌐ improves-ments, ⟍ whether, ⟍ practice-d, ⟍ practicable, ∫ especial-ly, ⌐ commercial-ly, ⟍ financial-ly, ⌐ questionable-ly, ⌐ uniform-ly-ity, ⌐ unanimous-ly, ⌐ executive, ⌐ defective, ⋀ republic, ⋀ republican.

LESSON XIII. ⌐ accord-ing *or* according to, ⌐ cared, ⌐ guard, ⌐ great, ⌐ called, ⌐ equalled *or* cold, ⌐ gold, ⌐ cannot, ⌐ gentleman, ⌐ gentlemen, ⌐ particular, ⌐ opportunity, ⌐ build-ing, ∫ told, ⌐ tried, ⌐ trade *or* toward, ⌐ towards, ⌐ third, ⌐ short, ⌐ spirit, ⌐ hand, ⌐ under, ⌐ yard, ⌐ word, ⌐ school, ⌐ schooled, ⌐ immediate, ⌐ expenditure.

LESSON XVI. ⟋ rather *or* writer, ⟋ wonderful-ly, influential-ly, character, characteristic, interest, respect-ed, respectful, prejudice-d-ial, advertise-d-ment, telegram, telegraphic, arbitrate, arbitrary, arbitration, discharge-d, certificate.

LESSON XV. peculiar-ity, probable-ly-ility, instructive, instruction, inconsiderate, enlarge, enlarged, enlargement, selfish-ness, inscribe-d, inscription, production, reproduction, objection, introduction, demonstrate, demonstration.

LESSON XVI. nevertheless, notwithstanding, perform-ed, performs-ance, efficient-ly-cy, sufficient-ly-cy, deficient-ly-cy, proficient-ly-cy, inspect-ed-ion, expensive, distinguish-ed, relinquish-ed, appointment, emergency.

LESSON XVII. proportion-ed, proportionate-ly, description, capable, electric, electrical, electricity, magnetic-ism, individual-ly, whatever, whenever, intelligent-ly, intelligence, intelligible-ly, investigation, investment, Parliamentary.

Lesson XVIII.   bankruptcy,   cross-examine-d
-ation,   England,   English,   enthusiastic-iasm,
familiar-ity,   familiarize,   inconvenient-ce,
incorporated,   indispensable-ly,   mortgage-d,
neglect-ed,   negligence,   legislative,
legislature,   organizer,   preliminary,
reform-ed,   universe,   prospectus.

Lesson XIX.   govern-ed,   government,
manufacture-d,   manufacturer,   exchange-d,
independent-ly-ce,   sensible-ly-ility,   maximum,
minimum,   universal,   mechanical-ly.

GRAMMALOGS

(IN THE LESSONS)

Arranged alphabetically

The numbers given before each word indicate the number of the Lesson in which the word occurs.

A

1 a
13 accord
13 according
13 according to
10 advantage
1 all
1 an
1 and
3 any
4 are
2 as
5 as is
1 aught
1 awe

B

10 balance
1 be
5 because
10 been
10 behalf
8 belief
8 believe
8 believed
6 beyond
13 build

13 building
1 but

C

8 call
13 called
2 can
13 cannot
8 care
13 cared
11 circumstance
13 cold
2 come
4 could

D

8 dear
8 deliver
10 deliverance
8 delivered
8 delivery
2 difference
2 different
10 difficult
2 do
8 doctor

7 dollar
7 dollars
8 during

E

8 equal
13 equalled
8 equally

F

4 first
2 for
9 from

G

10 general
11 generalization
10 generally
13 gentleman
13 gentlemen
2 give
2 given
2 go
13 gold
13 great
13 guard

H		1 it		6 Oh !	
2 had		5 itself		1 on	
13 hand				10 opinion	
2 has		**J**		13 opportunity	
2 have		11 justification		1 ought	
6 he				4 our	
3 him		**L**		5 ourselves	
4 himself		3 language		9 over	
2 his		2 large		6 owe	
4 hour		8 largely		3 owing	
6 how		8 larger		3 own	
9 however		8 liberty			
				P	
I		**M**		13 particular	
12 importance		3 me		8 people	
12 important		8 member		9 pleasure	
12 impossible		9 mere		8 principal	
12 improve		9 more		8 principally	
12 improved		4 most		8 principle	
12 improvement		9 Mr.		1 put	
3 in		2 much			
4 influence		4 myself		**Q**	
4 influenced				4 quite	
11 information		**N**			
15 inscribe		9 near		**R**	
15 inscribed		4 next		14 rather	
15 inscription		9 nor		9 remark	
15 instruction		10 northern		9 remarked	
15 instructive		8 number		8 remember	
2 is		8 numbered		8 remembered	
5 is as					
		O		**S**	
		6 O !		11 satisfaction	
		1 of		13 school	

13 schooled		4 that		**V**		
15 selfish		1 the		9 valuation		
15 selfishness		9 their		9 very		
4 sent		3 them		**W**		
5 several		5 themselves		3 was		
3 shall		9 there		3 we		
13 short		9 therefore		6 what		
1 should		3 thing		6 when		
10 significance		2 think		12 whether		
10 significant		13 third		2 which		
11 signification		5 this		1 who		
10 signified		5 those		3 whose		
10 signify		3 though		6 why		
10 southern		5 thus		3 wish		
7 speak		8 till		6 with		
7 special		1 to		10 within		
7 specially		1 to be		4 without		
13 spirit		13 told		14 wonderful		
11 subject		1 too		14 wonderfully		
11 subjected		13 toward		13 word		
11 subjection		13 towards		6 would		
11 subjective		13 trade		14 writer		
9 sure		13 tried		**Y**		
8 surprise		8 truth		13 yard		
8 surprised		1 two		3 year		
T		**U**		6 you		
8 tell		13 under		3 young		
2 thank		3 usual		3 your		
2 thanked		3 usually				

CONTRACTIONS

(IN THE LESSONS)

Arranged alphabetically

These lists of Contractions do not contain all of the words which may be contracted in accordance with the directions given in Lesson XX of the *New Era Course.* A few examples of such words are given, however, as a reminder to the student of the rules for contracting similar words. [A prefix or a suffix may be attached to a contracted form; as ⟍ *productive,* ⟋ *reproductive;* ⋀ *respect,* ⋀ *respectful,* ⋀ *disrespectful.*]

A

6 acknowledge

6 acknowledged

20 administrate

20 administration

20 administrative

14 advertise-d-ment

7 altogether

5 anything

16 appointment

14 arbitrary

14 arbitrate

14 arbitration

20 assignment

B

18 bankruptcy

C

17 capable

14 certificate

14 character

14 characteristic

11 circumstantial

12 commercial-ly

20 contingency

18 cross-examine-d-ation

D

20 danger

12 defective

16 deficient-ly-cy

15 demonstrate

15 demonstration

17 description

20 destruction

10 difficulty

14 discharge-d

16 distinguish-ed

183

E

16 efficient-ly-cy

17 electric

17 electrical

17 electricity

16 emergency

18 England

18 English

15 enlarge

15 enlarged

15 enlargement

20 entertainment

18 enthusiastic-iasm

12 especial-ly

7 establish-ed-ment

19 exchange-d

12 executive

7 expect-ed

13 expenditure

16 expensive

F

18 familiar-ity

18 familiarize

7 February

12 financial-ly

G

19 govern-ed

19 government

I

13 immediate

20 imperfect-ion-ly

15 inconsiderate

18 inconvenient-ce

18 incorporated

19 independent-ly-ce

18 indispensable-ly

17 individual-ly

14 influential-ly

11 inform-ed

11 informer

16 inspect-ed-ion

7 insurance

17 intelligence

17 intelligent-ly

17 intelligible-ly

14 interest

15 introduction

17 investigation

17 investment

7 irregular

20 irrespective

11 irresponsible-ility

J

7 January

K

6 knowledge

L

18 legislative

18 legislature

M

17 magnetic-ism

19 manufacture-d

19 manufacturer		14 prejudice-d-ial-ly	
20 manuscript		18 preliminary	
19 maximum		15 probable-ly-ility	
19 mechanical-ly		15 production	
19 minimum		20 productive	
18 mortgage-d		16 proficient-ly-cy	

N

18 neglect-ed		17 proportion-ed	
18 negligence		17 proportionate-ly	
7 never		20 prospect	
16 nevertheless		18 prospectus	
6 New York		11 public	
5 nothing		11 publication	
16 notwithstanding		11 publish-ed	
7 November			

O

Q

20 object-ed		12 questionable-ly	
15 objection			

R

20 objective		18 reform-ed	
20 obstruction		7 regular	
11 organization		16 relinquish-ed	
11 organize-d		9 remarkable-ly	
18 organizer		20 remonstrate	

P

17 parliamentary		11 represent-ed	
20 passenger		11 representation	
15 peculiar-ity		11 representative	
16 perform-ed		15 reproduction	
16 performs-ance		12 republic	
12 practicable		12 republican	
12 practice-d		14 respect-ed	
		14 respectful	
		20 respective	
		11 responsible-ility	

S

11 satisfactory

19 sensible-ly-ility

5 something

11 subscribe-d

11 subscription

16 sufficient-ly-cy

20 suspect-ed

T

14 telegram

14 telegraphic

7 together

U

12 unanimous-ly

7 unexpected

12 uniform-ly-ity

19 universal

18 universe

5 United States

W

17 whatever

17 whenever

Y

7 yesterday

ADDITIONAL CONTRACTIONS

A

abandonment
abstraction
abstractive
administrator
administratrix
amalgamate
amalgamation
arbitrator
attainment

C

contentment

D

dangerous
democracy-atic
denomination-al
destructive
destructively

E

enlarger
enlightenment
everything
executor
expediency
extinguish-ed

F

falsification
familiarization

I

identical
identification
imperturbable
irrecoverable-ly
irremovable-ly
irrespectively

M

marconigram
mathematical-ly
mathematician
mathematics
messenger
metropolitan
ministration
ministry
misfortune

O

obstructive

P

performer
perpendicular
perspective
project-ed
prospective
publisher

R

recoverable
reformer
remonstrance
remonstrant
removable
respectively

S

stranger
substantial-ly
sympathetic

U

unanimity
university
unprincipled

FIFTY CITIES AND TOWNS OF CANADA

Arranged alphabetically

Belleville (Ont.)		Ottawa (Ont.)	
Brandon (Man.)		Peterboro' (Ont.)	
Brantford (Ont.)		Port Arthur (Ont.)	
Calgary (Alta.)		Prince Albert (Sask.)	
Charlottetown (P.E.I.)		Quebec (Que.)	
Chatham (Ont.)		Regina (Sask.)	
Dawson (Yukon)		Rossland (B. C.)	
Edmonton (Alta.)		St. Catharines (Ont.)	
Fort William (Ont.)		St. Henri (Que.)	
Fredericton (N. B.)		St. Hyacinthe (Que.)	
Guelph (Ont.)		St. John (N. B.)	
Halifax (N. S.)		St. Thomas (Ont.)	
Hamilton (Ont.)		Sarnia (Ont.)	
Hull (Que.)		Saskatoon (Sask.)	
Kingston (Ont.)		Sherbrooke (Que.)	
Lethbridge (Alta.)		Stratford (Ont.)	
London (Ont.)		Strathcona (Alta.)	
Medicine Hat (Alta.)		Sydney (N. S.)	
Moncton (N. B.)		Three Rivers (Que.)	
Montreal (Que.)		Toronto (Ont.)	
Moose Jaw (Sask.)		Vancouver (B. C.)	
Nanaimo (B. C.)		Victoria (B. C.)	
Nelson (B. C.)		Windsor (Ont.)	
New Westminster (B. C.)		Winnipeg (Man)	
Niagara Falls (Ont.)		Woodstock (Ont.)	

PROVINCES AND DISTRICTS OF CANADA

PROVINCES

Alberta (Alta.)

British Columbia (B. C.)

Manitoba (Man.)

New Brunswick (N. B.)

Nova Scotia (N. S.)

Ontario (Ont.)

Prince Edward Island (P. E. I.)

Quebec (Que.)

Saskatchewan (Sask.)

DISTRICTS

Franklin

Mackenzie

Yukon

Keewatin

Ungava

INDEX

The figures refer to the paragraphs except where the page is mentioned

PRINTED IN GREAT BRITAIN AT THE PITMAN PRESS, BATH
z—(445)